Beds and borders

 AREND JAN VAN DER HORST

INTRODUCTION BY RICHARD ROSENFELD

 **REBO** PRODUCTIONS

© 1996 Rebo Productions, Lisse
© 1997 Published by Rebo Production Ltd
Text: Arend Jan van der Horst
Cower design and lay-out: Ton Wienbelt, The Netherlands
Photo editing: TextCase, The Netherlands
Translation: Suzanne Walters for First Edition Translations Ltd, Great Britain
Typesetting: Hof&Land Typografie, The Netherlands

ISBN 1 901094 34 0

Contents

	Foreword	5
CHAPTER 1	A brilliant whirl of colour: red, orange, and blue	6
CHAPTER 2	The green and white garden	14
CHAPTER 3	Grey with pink, yellow, and white	28
CHAPTER 4	Blue, pink, and purple	40
CHAPTER 5	Decprative foliage	72
CHAPTER 6	Perennials in place of weeds	123
	Photo credits	141

Foreword

Everyone thinks beds and border, and no argument, must be scaled-down copies of the great grand borders they see at the grandest gardens. You know, the horticultural equivalent of the team photograph, with the smallest plants at the front, bright eyed and bushy tailed, everyone knowing their place, and the tallest, most frightfully important plants at the back, roses and clematis, and sweet peas climbing up wigwams. Even non-gardeners know, by a kind of omnipresent energetic osmosis, that beds and borders are proper.

Which is exactly what I thought until I visited a private French chateau, an hour from Paris, where the owner – a tall angular man, an artist who used to run round the garden naked in a full moon, and who was the illegitimate child of a great 19th century novelist – had created a sequence of wholly original borders, turning tradition on its head.

Looking down on the garden from an upstairs window you could see three, short, slim beds in the middle of the lawn, pointing away from the house, one just to the left, one to the right, and one straight ahead. And after a few steps, six slightly longer ones, like arrows pointing away, and then another gap, followed by what I can only describe as a whole horde of them, all getting longer and more colourful the further they were from the house, pointing towards the river.

On close-up you realized that the smallest were very Victorian, packed with olive grey echeverias, and purple alliums with their enormous pom-pom flowers. The next group was a tapestry or cacophony of geraniums, clashing magenta, white, pale pink and mauve which had not been kept seperate but trained to spread one through the other. And the longest borders broke all known rules. They were edged with feathery fennel, so you had to part them like a curtain to see what was happening within. One of the biggest had in the centre not the tallest plants, but the smallest, and a big cast iron bed where you could have a snooze surrounded by delphiniums and campanula.

Eccentric yes, but it was a brilliant lesson that a fixed desing simply does not exist. Beds and borders are what you want. In fact they are a relatively recent creation. In the 17th century they bore no relation to the great blockbusters of a Gertrude Jekyll. They were long and thin, with more soil than plants, where the latter were set out every few feet. This was because you were meant to appreciate every single part of them (stem, flowers, etc.), the plants having a strong novelty value, being fresh discoveries from the New World. The beds were a kind of outdoor display shelf.

Parterres edged with elaborately curved lines of box then became it to those who had land and money; the landscape style of the 18th century saw flowers replaced by parkland; and then, from the 1770s, flowers were back with a vengeance, their popularity both down to asthetics and the staggering range of new plants being ferried beck by the plant hunters.

The latest trend is away from cottage garden informality inside crisp paths and smart, geometric design, to informal drifts of native plants growing as they would in the wild. It's not so much a case of we inspecting them, as being permitted to walk amongst them.

The most important thing when designing beds and borders is being aware of all possibilities. And Arend Jan van der Horst, in this splendid new book, opens your eyes to that.

Richard Rosenfeld, East Sussex, 1997

A brilliant whirl of colour: red, orange, and blue

In very famous gardens, it was often painters who were responsible for the surprising colour effects found there.

To see how the queen of the English perennial flower bed, Gertrude Jekyll, mixed pink and purple with yellow and orange is an intriguing experience. She had noticed that long perennial borders soon start to look flat and sickly if you do not introduce some colour contrasts. I remember the border at Abbots Ripton, the splendid garden of Lord Ramsey, where a long sight axis had been drawn from the rear elevation deep into the garden, formed by a grass path with wide perennial borders to left and right. In these borders was a great deal of *Helenium* (the orange-brown 'Moerheim Beauty,' I believe), yellow *Ligularia dentata* 'Desdemona', *Ligularia przewalskii*, white phlox and a lot of blue *Salvia*, and globe thistle, *Echinops* – in other words all simple, well-known plants. Groups of violet-flowering *Phlox*, *Lythrum*, and *Geranium* had been inserted in strips to make the border – which must have been 60m (200ft) long - more fascinating. This is a lesson to take to heart and one which Gertrude Jekyll had learned as a water colour painter. One of the remarkable discoveries here is that some colours, like purple and blue, create depth. In paintings of landscapes and buildings, depth is added with purple and blue, as in flower paintings. So this is why the deep colours purple, blue, and violet are used in borders. A painter who applied this idea in a very distinct manner was Claude Monet, who constantly used his magnificent flower garden in Giverny as the subject of his paintings. The shadowy areas in his paintings of a border full of red

You can buy annual delphiniums and poppies in a meadow flower mixture and sow them on bare ground. If the ground remains bare, for example at the edge of a flower bed, they will grow again next year – otherwise grass will eventually push them out.

Canna and orange East Indian cherry are pure purple. The effect is dramatic and mysterious. Why should we not repeat this effect in the garden too, and plant blue globe thistle, *Echinops*, next to tall *Canna*, with lavender, *Lavandula angustifolia* 'Hidcote', next to the East Indian cherry? You can also work with the dark foliage of, for example, *Heuchera micrantha* 'Palace Purple', to give depth to a pink, blue, or white group of plants. Purple Labiatae, *Physostegia*, next to pink autumn anemone, *Anemone tomentosa*, for example, gives depth, while at the beginning of the summer purple cleome gives the same effect to the lighter purple honesty. Anyone can experiment like this with blue and purple next to lighter colours.

Claude Monet designed a colourful flower garden at his house in Giverny, France. Here it is pictured in spring with orange-red wallflowers.

Monet's border in Giverny

On the garden side of the pink-painted house with light green shutters is a light green flower garden. A number of large trees stand near the house, providing the necessary shade in the summer. Monet loved to eat outdoors and liked to spend a long time at the table, hence the shade right by the kitchen doors. A long, straight gravel path runs at right angles to the rear elevation into the flower garden. For three-quarters of the year there is a richly coloured feast for the eye beside this path. In the spring there are many red and purple tulips with matching violas. After that come peonies, irises, and roses. Tall *Eremurus*, foxtail lily, follows in height the phlox, which bloom here for the second half of the summer. Every summer groups of East

This cockade-type flower is called Gazania. It lasts for several years and goes well in a multi-coloured flower garden. Euphorbia griffithii *'Fire Glow' with its soft orange flowers is in the foreground.*

Indian cherry were planted beside this straight path. This grew during the course of the summer into low round lobes which hung over the path. This gives a unique effect, which can be admired again now that the garden has been restored to its old glory and richness of flowers. The colours are varied, in a picturesque way, and depth and suspense are created by the colour contrasts. The wide rose arches, which Monet had erected over the two borders and the gravel path, give his garden a look all of its own. The arches are painted the same light green colour as the shutters of the house, and have acquired the climbing roses *Rosa* 'Golden Showers' and *R.* 'New Dawn', both long-flowering hardy specimens.

The combination is unique – who would put yellow next to pink? But it works, since both colours are soft. Blue wisteria has been trained over arches here and there for early flowering. The wisteria blooms at the same time as the irises, which changes everything into a blue symphony of colour.

Next to the house the path ends in a large round flower bed which is always filled with colour. This is where they ate, so it was constantly under view. It is easy to see why the painter had large glasshouses, in which he cultivated large plants in pots so that, as soon as one group had finished flowering, he could put in a new patch of colour. In summer the bed has *Canna* with geraniums. In the spring it is a sea of

Bij Great Dixter in het dorpje Northiam, Engeland, heeft Christopher Lloyd een gemengde border samengesteld met veel grijzen op de achtergrond, waardoor de oneindigheid van verten overloopt in lucht en landerijen.

red and pink tulips, which look very cheerful beside the pink house, and not at all ugly.

Standard roses, mostly in tints of violet and pink, stand at the back of the borders to give tall colour. Roses bloom for a long time and are a great mainstay for lovers of colour. Standard roses are also ideal for giving height. They can be planted happily in between the perennials, as Monet shows us.

If your border is long, you can repeat groups, for example groups of lady's mantle at the front of the border. You can do the same thing with bushes or cluster roses, or foliage plants such as *Hosta*, *Stachys*, and *Nepeta* (catmint). Lavender can be repeated in groups at the front, especially as its grey foliage remains interesting in the winter, introducing some welcome colour.

In Monet's day people were not particularly interested in grey tints; this idea came from Gertrude Jekyll and, after her, Margery Fish, who both mixed a great deal of grey in their borders. Margery Fish even had a nursery of grey plants in the garden of her house, East Lambrook Manor, Somerset. An *Artemisia* discovered by her is named 'Lambrook Silver,' after this romantic, magnificent garden! Elizabeth, the Queen Mother, used to come here regularly to buy plants for her grey garden at Windsor Castle. Mixing roses in borders is an English fashion.

This border of annuals is beautifully varied and is constantly colourful. African marigolds, Gazania, orange-yellow and pink begonias . . . it is certainly multi-coloured and the answer for anyone who does not want a sombre garden.

Groups of golden rod, *Solidago, Phlox, Helenium,* and *Salvia nemorosa* can form the centre of the border, with the very tallest perennials, such as *Aruncus* (goat's beard), *Echinops* (globe thistle), and *Eupatorium* at the back. Most types of *Ligularia* also grow tall and are suitable for repeating in groups with their bright yellow flowers. Many yellow plants are suitable for repetition, since yellow stands out, like white.

In planning a multi-coloured border you should always make sure that you start with plenty of deep colours like orange, dark blue, yellow ochre, deep violet, wine red, and bright violet as a base. Lighter groups of the same tints are put with them, and very light colours, such as marguerite daisies, white *Centranthus,* light pink *Geranium endresii,* and *Anaphalis triplinervis* can be planted in patches at the front and among the dark coloured tall perennials to brighten them up. Making a good multi-coloured border is a true art and actually much more difficult than a coloured border restricted to one or two colours.

What you can plant One of the most fascinating borders I know was designed by the gardening writer Christopher Lloyd, who writes his many books at his house, Great Dixter. The garden is old and was laid out by his father with topiary, yew gateways, and crenellated hedges. Walls have been extended from the old house as space-dividing elements. Christopher

Astilbe *'Fanal' is wine red, while* Lysimachia punctata *is yellow. Behind them stand the tall yellow spikes of* Ligularia przewalskyi.

Lloyd has laid a long border, the whole of which faces south. In front is a wide flagstone path. Numerous yellow, red, orange, and purple colours have been incorporated into the border itself. I remember tall red roses, pink fleabane *(Erigeron)* in a short variety, yellow *Ligularia*, orange *Alstroemeria*. Shrubs with purple and grey foliage have been placed in the background. There are *Berberis* with red foliage and grey willows, and tall yellow broom and roses such as *Rosa sericea (R. omeiensis)* which has large rosehips and large purple-red thorns. The combination of the shrubs with either their purple or grey foliage waving in the wind, including *Buddleia,* makes a unique background full of contrast. Visitors almost always take in this border step by step. At the end is a corner bench, from which you can look along the border as it moves in the wind. A *Taxus* hedge has been put behind the border on the north side as background; on the south side lies an open meadow. This is therefore a single, not a double, border.

The lavender-blue Polemonium caeruleum *is combined here with* Euphorbia palustris.

The multi-coloured border at The Priory

If you have studied colours to any extent, you will know that light consists of different colours which can be separated by a prism. A man once moved into a romantic (though austerely shaped) sand-coloured English house where he set about unravelling these colours and then interpreted them as a border. His house is called The Priory, the place Kemerton, and he himself is David Healing. He once told me that a long stay in a German prison gave him plenty of time to

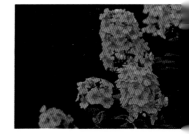

Phlox paniculata *hybrids come in bright or delicate tints. This is a bright 'Eclaireur'.*

read a book about the art of English gardening. It was written by William Robinson, an Irish landscape gardener who achieved great prosperity from publishing many books and the magazine, *The Garden*. In one of Robinson's books, *The English Flower Garden*, he describes how colours follow one another and how a border could be built up according to these principles. David Healing has now put this into practice. A long strip of ground facing north was chosen. A hedge formed the background, with a broad expanse of grass in front. The structure began with white, then came pink, purple, blue, then red and yellow, and this was repeated continually up to the end of the border. There were white roses, *Anaphalis*, *Centranthus ruber* 'Albus' and phlox, pink dahlias, phlox and roses, blue *Salvia*, *Aconitum*, and *Nepeta*, with dahlias, *Geranium psilostemon*, and *Phlox* 'Aïda' in violet. There were orange *Helenium* 'Moerheim Beauty' and *Alstroemeria*, and more roses and dahlias in deep red. The yellow of *Heliopsis*, *Rudbeckia*, *Helenium*, and *Oenothera* formed a warm centre with the red and orange. Throughout the whole border (which continued after this with orange, violet, blue, pink, and white again), annuals such as *Cosmea*, *Cleome*, and annual *Salvia* were also mixed in. This was one of the most fascinating borders I have seen.

Veronica spicata 'Alba' is the tall upright white variety, which is combined here with Telekia speciosa *with its large leaves and yellow marguerite-like flowers.*

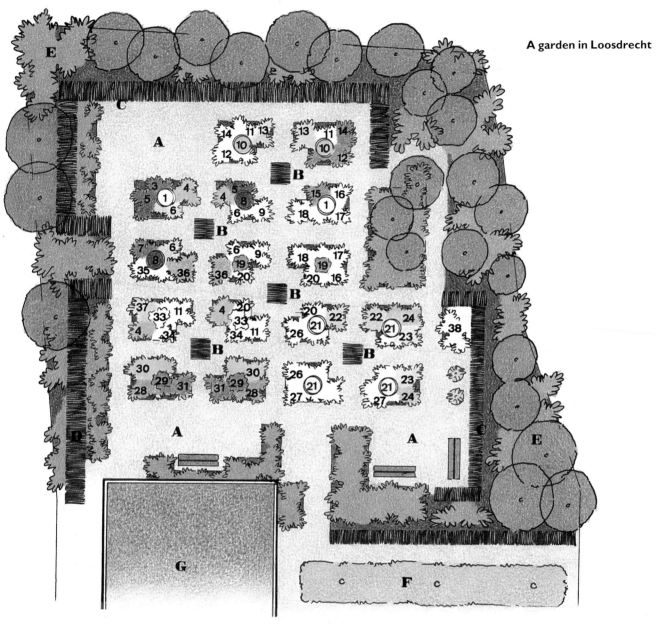

A garden in Loosdrecht

A	terraces	
B	wedges of box	
C	yew hedges	
D	beech hedges	
E	tall trees with shrubs	
F	car park with espalier limes	
G	house	

1   *Osmanthus burkwoodii*

2   *Campanula portenschlagiana*

3   *Lavandula angustifolia* 'Munstead'

4   *Gypsophila* 'Rosenschleier'

5   *Aconitum napellus*

6   *Rosa* 'Papa Meiland'

7   *Salvia officinalis*

8   *Hydrangea macrophylla*

'Mariesii Perfecta'

9   *Lysimachia ephemerum*

10   *Hydrangea macrophylla*
      'Bouquet Rose'

11   *Rosa* "Schneewittchen" (*Rosa* 'Iceberg')

12   *Pulmonaria saccharata* 'Mrs Moon'

13   *Astrantia major*

14   *Sedum* 'Herbstfreude'

15   *Centaurea montana* 'Grandiflora'

16   *Aster cordifolius* 'Silverspray'

17   *Iris pumila hybrid* 'Die Braut'

18   *Helianthemum* 'The Bride'

19   *Delphinium* 'Völkerfrieden'

20   *Geranium sanguineum* 'Album'

21   *Rosa* 'Peace'

22   *Acanthus mollis*

23   *Kirengeshoma palmata*

24   *Hosta crispula*

25   *Alchemilla mollis*

26   *Helleborus niger*

27   *Rosa* 'Swaney'

28   *Nepeta sibirica*

29   *Fuchsia longipendiculata*

30   *Geranium psilostemon*

31   *Salvia nemorosa* 'Mainacht'

32   *Campanula carpatica*

33   *Anemone hybrida* 'Honorine Jobert'

34   *Anaphalis triplinervis*

35   *Geranium endressii*

36   *Hedera helix* 'Arborescens'

37   lemon balm

38   *Crambe cordifolia*

13

The green and white garden

The idea of constructing gardens or sections of gardens in one colour is English. In her books, Gertrude Jekyll gives many examples of gardens designed in one colour.

Gertrude Jekyll created borders of blue with violet and browny tints, and also borders of silver and white. A great deal can be learned from just this combination of silver and white. White dominates, for instance, a space which is completely full of large white roses. White with grey in between prevents coarseness because there is always some grey to neutralize everything, whether at flowering times or not. This also creates contrasts in foliage colour. White with grey, in other words white flowers with grey foliage, is superior to the coarseness of green foliage. Fortunately, interest in silver-grey plants is increasing.

Yellow Alchemilla *on its own. Even the white comes not from the flowers but from the stones.*

Grey-leafed plants with white flowers

Artemisia is one of the perennial plants with grey foliage which are popular at the moment. This is a herb which grows wild in most countries. At many small harbours you will find a short silver-grey *Artemisia*, which likes sea water. This seems to me to be a general characteristic of Artemisia: these plants are often found close to the sea. In Bonifacio, a little centuries-old town on the southeast coast of Corsica, I also saw *Artemisia* growing on white rocks. The slopes were covered in a blanket of grey. It must have been *Artemisia abrotanum*, wormwood. This is a bitter herb which, according to all the herb books, belongs in the medicinal garden. I use it to give height amongst tall green perennials. It looks magnificent amongst tall white delphiniums, white bush roses, and white autumn anemones, because its growth is open and its branches can grow to a height of 2m (6ft) before the soft yellow flowers open. If you plant them in a herb border as part of your collection and for their grey foliage, it is a good idea to trim them or top them, as otherwise they will grow too tall and will fall over in the rain. In the garden of my farmhouse in Zeeland they stand next to the roses, which soon finish blooming. So the grey *Artemisia* leaves are important from mid-July.

Besides *A. abrotanum* there are many decorative varieties which have been discovered by breeders or garden lovers. *A. absinthium* 'Lambrook Silver' grows to a height of 80cm (32in) and has small finely incized leaves. My favourites for bushy effects are *A. arborescens* and *A. a.* 'Powis Castle', which has curly foliage. It is also 80cm (32in) tall. Less bushy, but ideal for weaving around other plants, is *A. absinthium* 'Silver Queen', the elegant stems of which grow through the bushes of perennials, in combination with the white-flowering *Phlox* 'Rembrandt', *Astilbe* 'Professor van der Wielen' (1.20m [4ft] tall), and *Gillenia trifoliata*. Suddenly little white flames appear, airily brightening everything up. *Artemisia ludoviciana* has broad, elongated leaves with shallow incisions on the edges. The plant grows to a height of 1.20m (4ft) and is just right for use in a group. There is a shorter variety, *A. l.* 'Valerie Finnis', which grows to 60cm (24in). A real acquisition is *A. schmidtiana*, which remains short and forms the most beautiful ground-level cushion you can imagine. It is therefore ideal in the foreground, with short roses, *Iberis*, white *Viola cornuta*,

A white border with Lysimachia ephemerum, which lights up the border with its little white candles. The border is in front of the yew hedge which has been trimmed into waves.

Ruta graveolens 'Jackman's Blue' has bluish leaves, as has Santolina chamaecyparissus 'Lambrook Silver'. There are also groups of blue-grey Hosta *and the white* Iris germanica *hybrid 'White Knight', which has pure white flowers.*

and as a group of silver-grey with *Anaphalis.* Several other varieties of *Artemisia. schmidtiana* are on sale, such as the even shorter 'Nana' and 'Silvermound', 10cm (4in) tall. *Anaphalis* is another good silver-grey plant, as is *Stachys olympica,* lamb's tongue, which has dark grey leaves. These plants are all suitable for the foreground.

Verbascum is useful to give height. *V. chaixii* 'Album' has felt-like, grey leaves and white flowers, while *V. olympicum* has yellow flowers and grey leaves. The flowering stems of the latter grow to a height of 2m (6ft).

Also tall, but less vertical, is *Eryngium giganteum,* which grows to a height of 1m (3ft). This thistle-like plant is grown for its silver-grey incised foliage. The stem spreads its branches widely and the silver-grey leaves appear underneath the green flowers. Numerous plants have grey-green foliage, such as *Phlomis,* which usually has yellow flowers. You see a great deal of *P. fruticosa,* in particular. *P. tuberosa* is browny red and 1m (3ft) tall.

All have greyish-green foliage. The same is found with two other plants, but these are bluey green: *Thalictrum flavum,* which grows to 2m (6ft) and *Lysimachia ephemerum,* whose foliage is a sort of sea-green colour. *Salvia argentea* is silver-grey and has large leaves, which give the plant its decorative value. The foliage is grey because of the long fine hairs which grow on it very close together, proving that dryness will not be a problem.

In the garden of The Priory at Kemerton, a man created his dream garden, inspired by a book about the principles of colour by William Robinson. Here you see the white corner, which later changes to pink, then blue (white Anemone *hybrid 'Honorine Jobert').*

Putting together white flowers with grey foliage

I usually begin with splendid leaf forms which remain fascinating until winter, for example those of *Artemisia*. *Anaphalis* also lasts well, as does *Hosta crispula* which has white leaf edges around a green central area. The flowers are purple, which can be a reason for cutting them out before they bloom. *Astilbe*, too, has splendidly incised leaves which have a decorative value after flowering. If you are looking for noticeable leaf shapes, the flowering groups of white *Phlox paniculata* hybrid 'Rembrandt', which have large round blooms, or *P. carolina* 'Mrs Lingard', which has a more elongated flower and grows to a height of 1m (3ft), are good choices. The deeply incised, rather fern-like leaves of *Cimicifuga racemosa* are almost indispensable in a white shady garden. The late-blooming white flower spikes are 1.80m (5ft 10in) tall. The foliage is compact and the flower spikes make the plant elegant and light.

Plants with simple leaf forms

Phlox has "normal" elongated leaves, like most roses, while *Astrantia major* has splendid leaves. The white-flowering Labiatae, *Physostegia virginiana* 'Summersnow' does not have distinctive foliage, although it is certainly not an ugly plant, with its incised leaves and its fresh green colour. *Papaver orientale* 'Perry's White' has white flowers and grey-green foliage, which has a decorative value even after flowering. *Monarda* 'Virgo', the white bergamot plant, has fresh green, rather elongated leaves, while the perennial mallow *Lavatera* 'Ice Cool',

'Iceberg' roses are combined here with clouds of lady's mantle, Alchemilla mollis. Agapanthus grows underneath and brings the white back down to the ground.

Left: Eryngyium *has many blue varieties, such as* planum, *light blue, planum 'Blue Dwarf', dark blue, and the silver-leafed* E.giganteum *which has greenish-white flower heads.*

17

Houttuynia cordata comes in various leaf colours. The flower is always white with a yellow point of stamens.

which grows to a height of 1.20m (4ft), blooms white and has greyish-green, slightly incised leaves. *Lavandula angustifolia* 'Alba', which has white flowers, also has grey leaves. The slightly grey elongated leaves of *Lysimachia ephemerum* are nondescript, but its white flowers provide decorative value. You could make endless lists of plants with striking leaves and plants with special blooms but nondescript leaves that clearly need the company of plants with grey or beautifully formed leaves. If you do not succeed in making such a list, keep some space between the groups of plants and mix in plants like *Artemisia absinthium* 'Silver Queen' which will weave itself in between the others. *Astrantia*, because it quickly spreads, is another plant which weaves and lightens with its slender stems and fine flowers. A plant which is not used very often is the white-flowering *Gaura lindheimeri*, which has long slender stems. These stems, which easily mingle with other perennial plants, grow to a height of 90cm (36in) and bear fine white flowers which follow each other in long succession. This is also a really good plant for weaving around others; you can put it in among the larger plant groups to create a cohesive, light effect.

White roses with white perennials

A method I often use to prolong the flowering in a white border is to plant white-flowering roses among the perennials. Favourites for this are easy-to-maintain cluster roses, because they do not require much

Green box shapes combine well with the delicate flowers of Erigeron, Geranium, *and* Astrantia.

The Anemone *hybrid*
'Honorine Jobert'
is white with a yellow
centre. It blooms from
August until the snow
falls.

pruning. *Rosa* 'Marie Pavic' blends easily with delicate perennials such as *Artemisia, Gillenia, Gaura,* and *Lysimachia ephemerum.* The roses have rather lobate leaves, which makes them look full, even though they are not. They grow about 60 to 80cm (24 to 32in) tall if they are pruned thoroughly once a year. *Rosa* 'White Fleurette' grows to about 1.50m (5ft) if it is not pruned too much. This is a small-flowered rose with an open, yellowy centre, which blooms throughout the whole summer. Cut the cluster away only when it has stopped blooming completely – not too deeply, because the new bloom cluster is already waiting to flower lower down. I have used *R.* 'Iceberg' a great deal because it presents no problems, blooms richly, and always appears to survive. *R.* 'Virgo' is strong and has large white flowers, which last well in the garden and in bouquets. *R.* 'Maria Mathilda', like 'Iceberg', is suitable for sturdy borders. In very refined combinations both these roses are rather out of place: their presence is too strong and they detract from the more subtle plants. So 'Marie Pavic' remains the favourite for its dreamy aura of old-fashioned romanticism. Plant *Artemisia,* white lavender, and other grey-leafed plants with roses. The white-edged *Mentha rotundifolia* 'Variegata' is also attractive. The middle of the leaves is green. This *Mentha* goes well in the white garden – and all herbs are useful for preventing diseases, especially with roses. White onions are perfect for protection against mildew, so plant these with roses. *Rosa* 'Little White Pet' is a short broad rose with

*I designed this white
garden for Claartje de
Gruyter in Vught.
The white flowers
were planted in eight
square beds divided by
box.
The greenery is
Artemisia ludoviciana.*

fabulous double small white flowers. It is also romantic, so it fits well with box globes, yew hedges, little arches with roses, and small flower and leaf forms. *Artemisia schmidtiana* is splendid with it, as is *Pulmonaria saccharata* 'Sissinghurst White', which has white flowers and beautiful white-flecked leaves. You can put *Gypsophila paniculata* behind it, or *Gillenia,* or *Gaura,* and right in the background *Cimicifuga racemosa* and *Astilbe* 'Professor Van der Wielen'. This rose, which also comes as a standard, is a delight to the eye. It can be repeated in the background but at a slightly higher level.

If you live in a cottage-style house or have an old barn you can plant a path with it, with aromatic herbs under the standard roses, such as Roman chervil, *Malva moschata* 'Alba', and white lavender. *Rosa* 'Yvonne Rabier' flowers naturally white, has clusters of small open flowers, and grows no taller than 60cm (24in). It is an easy rose which our grandparents had in their gardens, and with its fresh green foliage it gives a strong emphasis as a short plant in a garden of perennials. Plant sturdy plants with it, such as *Phlox* and white autumn anemone, *Anemone hybrida* 'Honorine Jobert', with *Mentha rotundifolia* 'Variegata' with its white-edged leaves to bring out the foliage. A group of *Hosta* with their white-edged large leaves is another sturdy accompaniment.

The rose with red stamens which form the centre of an elegant, slender, open pure-white flower is called 'White Wings'. Wine red lends itself to

White hortensia is combined here with Veronica spicata *'Alba': round and straight are a fascinating contrast.*

repetition, for instance with *Heuchera micrantha* 'Palace Purple', which has purple leaves and white flowers which are so fine looking as buds.

The white *Ajuga reptans* 'Alba' fits in here too, as its leaves take on a slightly purple colour in the summer. *Ajuga* is a rewarding plant which seems to be happy anywhere. Unfortunately not many people know that there is a white variety. This is a really early spring-flowering variety, which makes a good leaf contrast with *Dicentra eximea* 'Alba', as the *Dicentra* leaf is fernlike and fresh green, which contrasts well with the slender-growing *Rosa* 'White Wings'.

This Arum italicum *is bright orange red in the autumn, even in places where nothing else seems to want to grow.*

Rhythmically planted groups of roses

I like symmetry if it is not taken too far. If the shape of two borders situated opposite each other, for instance, is already symmetrical, you can either choose symmetrical planting or go deliberately for asymmetry to avoid too much severity and predictability. Symmetrical plantings need to be experienced as a fascinating rhythm, or sufficient suspense must be introduced in the planting to create something fascinating. Imagine groups of *Rosa* 'Iceberg' standing opposite each other. *Hosta crispula* is put in front of them, with two *Crambe cordifolia* in the background. Their tall flower stems spring up, and remain interesting afterwards with their large leaves. *Lysimachia ephemerum* can then neutralize the bushiness of the cluster roses as a vertical play on shape.

Drama is created by using tall overhanging branches. *Pyrus salicifolia* (as a bush or pruned) is suitable for drawing together the two borders situated on each side of a path. Their branches grow wide and start to trail. *Buddleia davidii* 'White Profusion' can also bring together the borders to the left and right of a path with its wide, slightly overhanging branches, on which the elongated flower spikes grow. *Elaeagnus angustifolia* is a silver-grey bush with a colour which lightens; it is large, broad, and easy, and it prunes well. Put them opposite each other at the end, and possibly also at the beginning, of a border. If you do not want to wait, have tall, wide arches made by a blacksmith, and grow white climbing roses over them, such as 'Wedding Day', 'Bobbie James', and 'Climbing Iceberg'. You could also grow white grapes, white *Clematis* and white wisteria on them. Any mundaneness will then disappear of its own accord.

I designed this flower garden, in which white and grey are the predominant tones, for a Norwegian lady. The standard rose is 'Iceberg', the short rose 'Maria Mathilda'.

Asymmetrical rose planting in a perennial border

Rosa 'Nevada', which grows 3m (10ft) tall, is planted in a corner of the border. In the other corner are three standard *Rosa* 'Iceberg' with *Rosa* 'Marie Pavic' underneath. After that the white perennial selection is planted, with the lowest point in the middle and the plants gradually getting taller along the sides. An advantage of this asymmetry is that it does not matter if something dies as it is quickly replaced with something else. This would be a nuisance in a symmetrical border. You have more freedom if you start from a basis of irregularity. Asymmetry

is more natural and causes more surprises, because the mind cannot anticipate it.

Fanciful symmetry at Castle Walenburg

You would think that a garden in which you have been working for more than eight years would to some extent become your "own". This ought to be the case at Castle Walenburg, and yet it is not so. I always walk around it full of admiration, realizing that my garden will never be like this. The personal vision of the owners, Mr and Mrs Cannemans, is only too obvious.

Consider, for instance, the two perennial borders situated opposite each other. They are full of white *Campanula persicifolia* 'Alba', which flowers only once with large, hanging, white calyxes. There are white autumn anemones, white hortensias, and every year some white spider flower *(Cleome)*. In front of these white perennials the rounded pink-flowering Bergenia has been planted next to the entrance from the round lawn. This seems illogical, but is certainly effective when the leaves overhang. Then there are yellow-flowering tree peonies, *P. lutea ludlowii,* the red-flowering bush *Calycanthus floridus,* and pink- and white-flowering *Ekianthus campanulatus,* also a tall bush.

The borders are therefore full of bushes, but in front and in between the space is filled with perennials. The effect is fullness with a purpose. If you walk through here from the castle, the round lawn is a relief,

I planted white ornamental onions as spring-flowering plants near a white farmhouse. Perennials and roses come later, all flowering in white tints.

23

though not in the sense of tranquillity but of space, as there are four golden elms there which are pruned into golden yellow pillars. These put an end to any tranquillity.

However, the whole thing exhibits such strong romantism that it is indisputably a Canneman garden. This is in fact the basic principle: the garden is kept as a museum where the atmosphere must be preserved as far as possible.

Buddleia davidii 'White Profusion' at the back on the right, combined with Phlox, Lysimachia, and Astrantia in white tints.

A white silent garden

Since the garden of Castle Walenburg attracts about 7,000 visitors annually during its open season, certain things in the garden have to be changed.

In one garden, the so-called silent garden, five round plant beds, in a rectangular piece of grass surrounded by hornbeam, were reserved for perennials and a few bushes. In the middle was a border with a little sandstone pillar. Roses grew around it and lady's mantle along the edge.

In the four other round borders, each situated in a corner, was a variety of the flowering snowball tree, *Viburnum plicatum* 'Mariesii', with forget-me-nots and ragged robin underneath it. And that was it. After June everything in the side borders had finished blooming, and the silent garden certainly was silent as visitors quickly walked through it. This is why we sacrificed the ragged robin; the forget-me-nots were left as underplanting after the golden elms. The ragged robin was removed

It takes a lifetime to create topiary like this.

from under the four *Viburnum* bushes, which kept dying and which never grew into identical bushes, and a selection of white perennials was planted. This included white perennial violets, *Viola cornuta* 'Wheatley White', short white *Astilbe, Heuchera micrantha* 'Palace Purple' with its leaves of different shades of purple, and short varieties of white bleeding hearts.

Never choose *Dicentra spectabilis* for short planting, but *D. eximea* 'Alba', which displays beautiful foliage for the whole summer and the autumn. I also planted my favourite fern, *Polystichum setiferum,* which spreads out splendid, felt-like evergreen hardy foliage. It was a success and, with the tulip 'Angelique,' made the middle border a feast in the autumn as well. In the rose border I planted *Rosa* 'Kathleen' with *R.* 'Leersum'. They all bloom pale cream, as does *R.* 'Penelope', which is also there. *Clematis vitalba* 'Alba' was grown around a little pillar.

The standard plumed hortensias, which died, were also replaced. They stood in a circle around the little pillar and changed colour magnificently in the autumn.

The white standard rose 'Iceberg', which is reliable and blooms all the time, was also put here. I let it run on into the garden of cutting flowers (which is joined to the silent garden) along the path which joins the two parts of the garden together visually.

White-flowering Yucca *is a good plant to combine with a sunny grey and white garden. The slightly bluish foliage is also of value in the winter.*

A white flower garden around an iron summer-house

A splendid iron summer-house was put up beside a large terrace in Heeswijk-Dinther. The terrace is an exhibition area for statues which the owners collect and sell. The summer-house is for "déjeuners à l'ombre", or meals in the shade. It is large and overgrown with white wisteria, *Wisteria sinensis* 'Alba'. Around it I planted all sorts of large groups of white-flowering plants: *Rosa* 'Virgo' with large white flowers, *Astilbe* 'Professor Van der Wielen' with tall flower plumes, and white *Hydrangea arborescens* fill the borders which are enclosed by box hedges.

A beech hedge has been placed around this white summer-house garden with four semicircular openings for the four gateways. Two beech topiary shapes have been placed as guards between the large terrace and the smaller summer-house terrace. These are *Fagus sylvatica* shapes, which can be obtained by patient training and pruning. Choose continuous straight stems which have branches all the way down and leave branches opposite each other at equal distances, and cut away everything in between. By bending and tying them you can create layers of beech leaves that has a medieval effect.

The summer-house has a roof consisting of two sections, which has been designed so that it can be covered with glass some times if the owners wish.

Not an everyday combination of annuals, coloured cabbage varieties, and house and orangery plants. As long as they are used with taste, surprising results can be achieved

A garden in Vught

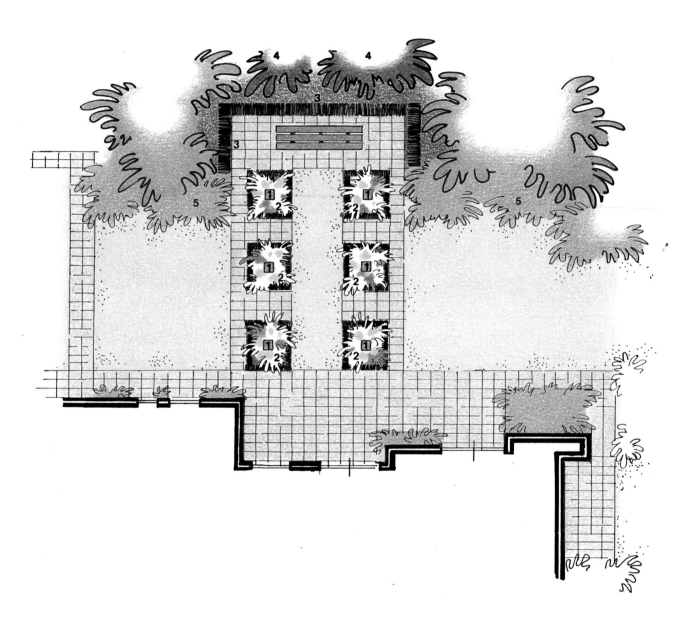

1 *Taxus baccata* pruned into obelisks

2 mixture of *Mentha rotundifolia* 'Variegata', *Phlox paniculata* hybrid 'Rembrandt, *Rosa* 'Iceberg', *Aster cordifolius* 'Silver Spray', and *Lilium candidum*

3 *Taxus baccata* hedge

4 two *Chamaecyparis lawsoniana* pillars

5 *Pachysandra terminalis* and other ground cover and globe shapes of *Osmanthus heterophyllus*

Grey with pink, yellow, and white

If you have ever visited any of the famous English gardens – those of Gertrude, Jekyll, for example – you will know that yellow and pink combine magnificently with soft grey.

I was summoned to England years ago to help to find illustrative material for a book on the Dutch and English gardens of William III and Mary. I took advantage of the opportunity to visit a good friend, a correspondent for *Country Life*. He took me to a large fascinating garden in Hertfordshire with the bizarre name of Bennington Lordship Garden. The house is sand-coloured and much of the paving in this park-cum-garden surrounded by numerous gardens is the same colour. The main materials are sandstone paving stones and gravel with yellowy loam. There is a rose garden, and a panoramic landscape in the style of Humphrey Repton, one of England's most influential landscape gardeners, who was a master of both landscape and the small garden style. It has spinneys, banks, and grass as far as the eye can see. A splendid rock garden comes as a surprise at the end of the formal flower garden. A large pond is divided into levels with blocks of flagstone, and planted with *Astilbe, Ligularia,* and *Tradescantia.*

Between the large formal vegetable garden and the rock garden is a long wide border. One side is enclosed by a wall, as it should be with kitchen gardens. I have a strong feeling that this wall was formerly used for espalier fruit. Now, however, apart from a single remaining espalier pear, roses grow against the pale brown walls, with botanical roses and Crambe in front. Beside the central path lady's mantle, *Alchemilla,* alternates with silver-leafed, purple-flowering wallflowers, *Erysimum* 'Bowles' Mauve', which bloom early in the spring. Groups of *Geran-*

Allium aflatunense is light purple, A. giganteum deep purple. Ornamental onion is combined here with dill, and is very refreshing in an informal mixture of colour.

CHAPTER 3   BEDS AND BORDERS

ium psilostemon, deep violet with a black centre, outshine everything here and are strikingly combined with the day-lily, *Hemerocallis*, with its elongated leaves. In the border you can also see white marguerite daisies, white *Papaver orientale* 'Perry's White', and white lupins.

As well as purple and white tints, yellow ones are also in rich supply. For example there is *Lysimachia punctata*, used as a vertical accent with its little yellow bells along its straight stems. *Aruncus dioicus*, a tall flowering plant with cream-coloured plumes, is also employed here. It is noticeable that not much blue is mixed in with these purple, yellow, and white tints. Delphiniums and irises in pale mauve colours provide a streak of colour. Groups coming from the back have been planted in small strips, so there is plenty to see at right angles to the direction of the path. This makes the whole border seem incredibly long. It has been raised slightly with blocks of sandstone to allow all the plants which bloom in a cloud-like fashion to hang airily over the path. Bush roses have been used in the background.

An unusual combination: pink with yellow

Numerous violet-coloured perennials bloom for a long time. These include *Geranium psilostemon*, purple loosestrife *(Lythrum)*, a great deal of fleabane *(Erigeron)*, all kinds of varieties of marjoram *(Origanum)*, *Phlox paniculata* varieties, *Thalictrum*, and a wide range of *Astilbe* varieties. In nature you often see violet next to yellow: *Lythrum* and marsh buttercup, *Ranunculus palustris*, at the edge of a ditch, and

Purple-blue Salvia nemorosa *is combined with pink poppies and yellow* Achillea *in this enormous border, the long, curving strips of which each have one variety of planting.*

the violet willow-herb, with wild *Hypericum,* in sandy areas. In dry regions of France wild violet perennial *Lathyrus* and yellow *Sedum acre* unite amicably. I have designed borders in these colour combinations several times and the result is thrilling. As a rule you use a great deal of violet with some yellow, or a great deal of yellow with some violet, just as in Bennington Lordship Garden. The large stretches of *Lysimachia punctata,* the many *Ligularia,* and the lady's mantle are yellow, while the *Geranium psilostemon,* the lupins, and bush roses are pink violet.

Pale pink gives a lift to an otherwise dark range of coulours.

Violet perennials *Allium schoenoprasum* 'Forescate' has bright pink-violet flowers, grows to 50cm (20in), and is a magnificent plant for the summer. *Aster ericoides* 'Cinderella', *A. e.* 'Esther,' and *A. e.* 'Ruth McConnell' all grow to a height of 80cm (32in) and bloom in the late summer. *Bergenia* 'Profusion' is violet pink. *Centranthus ruber* can also be included among the lilac-coloured flowers, although there is rather more brick-red in it. There are many bright pink carnations; *Dianthus deltoides,* in particular, is short and has a violet colour similar to an iris. The dull violet petals of *Epidemium rubrum* are fine, and this makes a good ground-cover plant under bushes or in a shady border. Cut off the foliage early in the spring, so you can enjoy the hundreds of tiny flowers. Many violet-flowering varieties of fleabane, *Erigeron,* are to be found. *Geranium psilostemon* is bright violet with a black

centre, while *Geranium pratense* is also violet, but short. *Psilostemon* grows to about 50cm (20in) in height.

There are more shades of violet to be found in *Geranium: G. endressii*, for example, is fresh violet pink. The little-known plant *Indigofera* has purply-pink flowers and *Lamium maculatum* 'Beacon Silver', which stays short, has purple-violet flowers and silver leaves. A bright violet tint is predominant in perennial sweet peas and in the wild *Lathyrus*. *Lavatera* 'Barnsley' is also violet, though on the light side, as are *Malva moschata* and many marjoram varieties. *Origanum laevigatum* 'Herrenhausen' is dark lilac, while the shorter *O. vulgare* 'Aureum' (25cm [10in]) has yellow foliage. *Scabiosa columbaria* 'Pink Mist' grows to a height of 40cm (16in) and has violet-lilac flowers. **Thalictrum delavayi** 'Hewitt's Double' grows tall, a good 1.5m (5ft), and has violet flowers on long stems above fine foliage. *T. aquilegiifolium* is the same, as is the variety *T. a.* 'Thundercloud', which blooms in the early summer. *Tricyrtus*, the orchid-like perennial from Japan, also has violet flowers, especially *T. formosa*. *Veronica spicata* 'Pink Damask', which has violet flowers, grows to a height of 60cm (24in). *Viola cornuta* is a strange variety, in which all the colours of the rainbow can be found. The *Allium* varieties, the purple *Centaurea* varieties, and *Filipendula purpurea* are plants that go well in a violet, yellow, and white border.

If you like wild plants you will be familiar with honesty, *Lunaria*

Hosta *and* Alchemilla mollis *add variety to each other and with only two shades provide an interesting contrast with the green in front and behind.*

Following pages: A large-leafed plant as a feature (that could perhaps be emphasized by a plant in a pot) livens up the planting.

31

annua, which is naturally violet in colour. They come up every year and have oval, silver seed pods as an autumn bonus.

These romantically overgrown arches divide various parts of the garden. One section of the garden has more yellow and the other has rather more pink and violet, while visually they both combine.

Roses with violet, white, and yellow

One of my favourite roses goes well with a violet garden. It is *Rosa* 'Betty Prior', a cluster rose which blooms continuously with a few bright violet flowers. As a climbing rose you can use *R.* 'Zéphirine Drouhin', which has no thorns and is bright violet. *R.* 'Rosa Mundi' (*R. gallica* 'Versicolor'), the apothecary's rose, is our oldest known rose, previously used in the kitchen and also for healing drinks and ointments, from which it gets the name apothecary's rose. Its colour is deep violet with a yellow centre. *R.* 'Bonica' is fresh light violet and blooms for a long time. There are other violet roses which go well with perennials. Of the yellow roses I prefer the pale yellow to the buttercup-yellow flowers. *R. hugonis* is good for the spring, *R.* 'Golden wings' as a tall long-flowering cluster rose, and *R.* 'Mermaid' as a climber with splendid open flowers and deep orange stamens.

Left: Here, with the pink Phlox paniculata *hybrid and yellow* Telekia, *and with* Chelone obliqua *further up, it is not so much a matter of varieties as of the "hazy" atmosphere.*

Water and marsh plants

Primula japonica spreads in marshes and at the damp water's edge. This candelabra primula comes in many tints of white and orange. Purple loosestrife was mentioned earlier as a wild violet plant. Many waterlilies are violet, and there are also some splendid yellow ones. Choose bright violet, light violet, and light yellow if you have a water garden next to your violet, yellow, and white border.

Violet-coloured borders

You will find violet flowers in *Hydrangea, Buddleia, Weigela,* and *Prunus* 'Accolade' – a small random selection from the enormous range that will go with a border of that colour. *Escallonia* and *Kolkwitzia* (which is more pinky violet) are softer. *Magnolia soulangiana* also has deep purple-violet colours. Let *Rosa* 'Cardinal de Richelieu' grow through one of these magnolias, and the little mauve-purple clusters will come through the summer-green foliage like dark streamers.

Dark-leafed plants with a violet garden

It seems almost too much of a good thing to plant violet-coloured foliage shrubs in addition to violet, yellow, and white flowers, but why should *Cotinus coggygria* 'Atropurpurea' or purple-leafed *Berberis* not look fascinating with bright purple? You can rear a purple-coloured hedge by planting *Fagus sylvatica* 'Purpurea'. This hedge goes with any colour, but it is still important to plant more purple-coloured plants, such as *Filipendula purpurea* and *Polygonum amplexicaule*. I prefer to see green hedges (such as holly and hornbeam) which repeat the green leaves of the bright flowering plants, and thus give the violet flowers a more natural balance.

The function of the separate colours

You only need a little white to maintain the link between violet and yellow in this colour combination. The fine white flowers of *Gaura, Gillenia,* the soap root *Gypsophila,* and many *Erigeron* varieties are splendid for this. The little flowers which appear thousands at a time on

The soft yellow of Anaphalis 'Schwefellicht' or of Santolina is a welcome break from the buttercup-yellow tints, which are combined with the blue of Geranium. Cerastium is a white-flowering perennial plant that will bloom a second time if the flower heads are removed after the first flowering. Veronica spicata 'Pink Damast' is combined here with Phlox.

33

the tall flower stems of *Crambe cordifolia* are also welcome, as are flowering shrubs with fine white flowers, such as *Deutzia, Exochorda, Spiraea,* and *Rubus tridel,* which blooms on elegantly curved branches.

**The function
of white**
White primroses, as well as white *Centranthus* and white honesty, can make things lighter when planted next to violet flowers of the same type. In the spring, white *Geranium phaeum* 'Album' forms a light bouquet which goes well with violet honesty, *Daphne mezereum,* and purple-violet *Aubrieta.* The large tufts of marguerite daisies in Bennington Lordship Garden stand well away from the white lupins and the white *Crambe,* forming lighter spots and nothing more in a sea of green, yellow, and violet.

**The function
of yellow**
Warmth is created by yellow. I often find too much yellow very heavy; this is why I use pale yellow colours initially. Lady's mantle and *Achillea taygetea* are both short to medium height. *Achillea* 'Credo' is sulphur yellow and grows to a height of 1.2m (4ft). There is a soft yellow variety of *Aconitum* too, *A. vulparia.* Hollyhocks have light yellow varieties, and the flowery curtains of *Angelica* are also pale yellow. These curtains of flowers are like those of lovage, *Levisticum officinale,* which can grow to a height of about 2m (6ft) and is useful as an ornamental plant in the background and as a culinary herb. *Anthemis* include marguerite-like flowering perennials: *A. tinctoria*

'E. C. Buxton' for instance, which grows to a height of 70cm (28in) and has soft yellow flowers. *A. t.* 'Wargrave' is also soft yellow and slightly taller at 1m (3ft). *Aquilegia chrysantha* is the name of the soft yellow 70cm (28in) tall perennial yellow columbine. *Aquilegia fragrans* is creamy white. For the spring and for shorter emphasis, there is *Epimedium,* two varieties of which have yellow flowers, *E. versicolor* 'Sulphureum', which is sulphur yellow and short (30cm [12in]), and *E. warleyense* 'Ellen Willmott,' which has brass-yellow flowers.

Euphorbia, which you can get in every shade from sulphur yellow to pale and bright yellow, is a "must" for every garden. Formerly one saw only the bright yellow *E. polychroma.* There are, however, varieties with coloured foliage, such as *E. characias* and the *E. amygaloides* varieties. *E. a.* 'Purpurea' has purple foliage and greeny yellow flowers. *E. characias* has reddish foliage, at least when it sprouts, and the same colour flowers, as do *E. dulcis* and *E. d.* 'Chameleon'. The many splendid varieties justify in every way planting a selection. It is worth mentioning, as a contrast, the tall yellow-flowering plant, fennel, which has fresh green leaves and blooms with showers of yellow flowers. A brown-leafed variety (or rather greeny-brown), *Foeniculum vulgare* 'Giant Bronze', also has yellow flowers and grows to a height of 2m (6ft). This is a beauty, although it does not go very well with violet, but you can always try it. The shape of the plant is, in any case, worth it.

Kirengeshoma palmata is a shade-loving plant with splendidly incised

It is difficult to think of anything to go with yellow conifer hedges. The borders are successful here for a number of reasons. The lively, diverting colour of bright violet has been introduced in the phlox, and is combined with soft pink tints.

foliage which blooms with little yellow bells. If it is not too dry and sunny for it, it grows to 80cm (32in), and *K. koreana* to 1m (3ft). At nurseries you will see many more light yellow plants. *Cephalaria gigantea*, which grows to a height of 2m (6ft), is a "must" for the violet and yellow garden with its strong slender stems and soft yellow scabiosa-like flowers. Or you may fall for the soft yellow *Helianthus decapetalus* 'Lemon Queen', which also grows to almost 2m (6ft). The light yellow *Scabiosa lucida* is a valuable decorative addition. This has a slender and swaying air, as has *Thalictrum flavum*. This *Thalictrum* grows to a good 2m (6ft), has blue-green foliage, and fluffy lemon-yellow flower clusters.

Here is a tip for lazy gardeners: plant the soft yellow-flowering **Tellima** and you will get rid of short weeds in no time. Sow *Verbascum* in amongst this, such as 'Gainsborough', which grows to a height of 1.2m (4ft). There are many wild mulleins, such as the silver-leafed Aaron's rod, *V. thapsus. Coreopsis verticillata* 'Moonbeam' blooms profusely with lemon-yellow, star-like flowers. It blooms for a long time in the late summer, the 50cm (20in) tall flowers appearing on slender stems.

Pink on its own is very tempting, but in very large gardens it soon becomes sickly and rather boring. Therefore the yellow of Euphorbia, Achillea ptarmica, and lady's mantle has been added, which is an ideal combination with pink. Lemon yellow tints combine perfectly with pink and blue.

A pink, violet, yellow, and white border for a small garden

Put short violet plants, such as *Sedum spurium* 'Schorbusser Blut' and its yellow relation *S. kamtschaticum*, in the foreground; then two clumps of lady's mantle, one on each side at the front, with *Geranium psilostemon* behind it. In the middle put the long-flowering *Geranium*

endressii, one plant of which is sufficient. In the central area you can have *Euphorbia characias* with its red foliage and yellowy green flowers which you should cut off in the summer, with *Helleborus* on each side of it as a dark violet spring-flowering plant. *Lythrum, Phlox paniculata* hybrid 'Aïda', violet *Rosa* 'Betty Prior', and soft yellow *Aconitum vulparia* can fill the central area, with *Cephalaria, Helianthus decapetalus* 'Lemon Queen', and the soft yellow *Rosa* 'Golden Wings' at the back of the border. Here you have a basic lay-out which can be extended in all sorts of ways with white in the foreground: plant *Gillenia, Gaura,* and the white *Phlox paniculata* hybrid 'Rembrandt' with white *Viola cornuta* 'Victoria Cawthorne'. Amongst the taller white flowers, *Veronica spicata* 'Alba' is good and reliable, with its upright points of white that grow to 1.8m (5ft 11in).

If there is more room and the border is deeper, you can have botanical roses, long-flowering David Austin roses, and also shrubs in yellow, violet, and white. *Cornus florida,* which blooms early in the spring, can be given a place, together with *Escallonia, Weigela,* and *Viburnum bodnantense* 'Dawn', which starts flowering in the winter. If you want extra drama you can make arches with roses, the red-leafed grape *Vitis vinifera* 'Purpurea', and the yellow *Clematis tangutica.* You can vary things by having a different emphasis each year, which often happens anyway as the result of drought, unruly growth, cold, and heat. Nature makes sure the garden changes every year.

Rosa *'Golden Showers' is yellow, while the grey cushion flowers later in pink. Above the grey foliage the wealth of flowers of* Teucrium chamaedrys *appears*

Blue, pink, and purple

The colours blue, pink, and purple are regarded as the classics of the perennial border. It is easy to see why. Few tints go together so harmoniously.

Many examples of the blue, pink, and purple colour combination are to be found in both English and Dutch gardens, for example in the two borders of Castle Walenburg. From my intensive involvement with these many times a year, together with the permanent gardener, Teus Mandersloot, and Paula Keijzer, who keeps an eye on the garden planting, it has occurred to me that certain rules apply. First of all there is the classic structure: tall plants behind, medium height ones in front of them, then shorter plants in front of them, and very short plants in the foreground. One way or another, however, there always seems to be a whirl of more or less equal-sized plants, with a taller group or a single plant now and then to prevent flatness. A continual effort has to be made to avoid the obvious. So no sections (as often seen in books) have just exactly the right compartment for every kind and variety of plant. To increase this informality certain plants weave in and out amongst the others and some single plants have been positioned in unusual places. This is a good lesson to learn: start with rather boring planting in groups and then do something imaginative to make sure you have sufficient variety.

Plants always want to grow outwards, where they think they will encounter more light and nourishment and thus grow bigger. This happens at the expense of neighbouring plants, which want to do the same but perhaps have less growing power. Without interference some plants will grow too large and others will disappear. So always keep to

Lavatera *comes in pink and violet. This is 'Barnsley', which has become popular because of its endless flowering, elegant growth, and colour, which seems to go well with everything.*

the original plan for the desired variety. You always need to reclaim space for delphiniums, for example. *Phlox, Geranium,* and *campanula* grow profusely on clay, so you have to make room (year in year out) for the delphiniums which are always getting broken. This is the price you have to pay to maintain variety. Lesson one is: maintain variety.

Lesson two is: make sure that, as well as all the green of the perennials, there are also effects which make things "airy". There is, of course, no question of real airiness in full borders, but the effect can be simulated with *Salvia sclarea,* with its greyish foliage and tall stems full of pink and purple flowers. *Artemisia, A. arborescens* 'Powis Castle', is included every year in the front of the border to introduce grey amongst the green. The third element is hosta, with blue foliage or foliage with white edges, which is repeated in groups amongst all the green. Slender-growing plants are allowed to rise above the mass of plants. One example is *Knautia,* the purple-coloured perennial which is similar to *Scabiosa;* others are *Gillenia* and *Thalictrum,* which suddenly shoots up as a tall plant amongst the short front section.

At Walenburg it is interesting to note that, though the two borders with grass between them have identical forms, they have a different overall appearance. Because of the differences in the way the light falls, there are always differences in growth, which result in a difference in size and

Large groups of pink and blue as basic colours. Phlox, Monarda, *and* Sedum *for the late summer are combined here with autumn asters and* Geranium.

41

which requires a different choice of planting. So in the south border you can have plants which catch the light if they receive the sun from behind. *Gillenia trifoliata* is one of these, as is one type of *Campanula lactiflora* 'Loddon Anna'. Plants with large leaves, such as *Hosta* and snakeweed, *Polygonum bistorta,* which blooms with long stems and little pink candles, give clarity at the front. The foliage remains splendid after flowering and is a decorative break from the finer plants. More 'Loddon Anna', *Cimifuga,* and *Phlox* stand in the background and shrub roses have been incorporated with them.

That is part of the secret of these borders; shrub roses have been given a permanent place. These tall, spreading, old-fashioned roses, known as shrub roses, grow to a height of about 2m (6ft) and are true mainstays whether in bloom or not. The green shapes are restful when fully grown, in bloom they add colour, and afterwards there is tranquillity again. They are kept upright with pieces of reinforced concrete which are placed together in threes, in the shape of a wigwam. *Rosa* 'Tuscany', *R.* 'Tuscany Superb', *R.* 'Oeillet Parfait', *R.* 'Reine des Violettes', *R.* 'St Nicholas', and *R.* 'Fantin Latour' have been planted against these.

The Canneman family used this idea when they lived at Hidcote Manor Garden, Gloucestershire, where new borders were laid in the kitchen garden and roses constituted an integral part of the background to the

Blue Salvia nemorosa *is combined splendidly here with pale pink poppies.* Lilium rubellum *has bell-shaped pink flowers and the centre is slightly darker.* Lilium wardii *lets its petals curl upwards, to create a turban shape*

perennial plant beds. Their flowering coincides with a high spot in the borders when most of the perennials are in bloom or just about to bloom. The many kinds and varieties of *Geranium* are also in bloom then, which gives an even, delicate effect.

Mr and Mrs Canneman have planted a veritable national collection of *Geranium*. There are *Geranium psilostemon* with its deep violet centre, *G. pratense* and *G. pratense* 'Mrs Kendall Clark', with its slightly greyish foliage, *G. macrorrhizum* 'Album', which blooms profusely but not for long, *G. m.* 'Spessart', and *G. nodosum*, which is kept to a minimum since this cranesbill will fill up prematurely all the gaps in the border with its light purple flowers. *G. platypetalum* is the last, a 40cm (16in) tall plant which has purple-blue blooms in a sea of slender flowers, and which spreads out into a bush.

Behind and next to the shrub roses there used to be large clumps of delphiniums: *Delphinium* 'Völkerfrieden', which has deep gentian-blue flowers, *D.* 'Finsteraarhorn', *D.* 'Blue Triumphator,' and *D.* 'Galahad'. The latter is a Pacific Giant hybrid, which flowers snow-white in long clusters, while *D.* 'Blue Triumphator' has violet-blue flowers. Because of the shade in the south border (created by large oak trees and bushes), there is a splendid diffuse light, but the delphiniums do not grow there any more. We still keep them going with difficulty amongst the other plants in the north border, which gets the sun, by

You can achieve this dreamy atmosphere by choosing fine-leafed plants without garish colours.

making gaps between all those turbulently growing perennials that try to take up all the available space. This is how nature would have it if we did not interfere, but people are always looking for variety.

After the delphiniums, the phlox family comes into bloom: *Phlox paniculata* hybrid 'Lilac Time', which is lilac-pink, and the white-flowering *P. p.* hybrid 'White Admiral'. They never fail to enchant, and neither does the *P. p.* hybrid 'Lavandelwolke', which grows several metres tall in the south border. The lilac original form of these phlox is called *paniculata*. All other varieties mentioned are descendants of this.

Garden marguerite daisies appear in the border on the south side: the *Chrysanthemum rubellum* hybrid 'Clara Curtiss', which blooms pure pink. In the corners of both the south and the north borders are bushes which bloom with tall white plumes; these are *Sorbaria aitchisonii*. This is a masterstroke, as the bushes grow to over 3m (10ft) tall, bloom with white plumes, and have fine foliage. But they need to be pruned drastically and intensively to give the hedges behind them a chance of survival. One thing which always strikes me is the planting of two kinds of *Polygonum*, *P. amplexicaule*, which blooms purple-carmine and *P. filiforme*, which appears in the north border with very thin spikes of carmine-red flowers.

Entering a garden is always an event of great significance. You often see doors thrown open on to a terrace, which has to be quite spacious for

Pink and blue are combined in this enormous border with lemon yellow. Salvia is purple-blue, while Sedum, Geranium, and Centranthus range from brick-red to pinky red and therefore combine well with yellow Alchemilla and Solidaster.

the large, comfortable garden furniture. Then the lawn unfolds with a single tree, which gives shade on warm summer days. The table and chairs are then moved into the shade on the grass, and from here you can see borders, bushes, and hedges.

There are several entrances at Walenburg. One is a purely visual one: from the castle you look across the terrace and over the moat towards the borders, with the spacious rectangular lawn to the right of the sight-line. The borders are to left and right, precisely along the sight-line.

As a second main entrance there is a long grass path with hedges of hornbeam along it. The path ends at two tall dawn redwoods, in front of which a bust has been placed. As you walk along the path you discover openings in the hedge on both sides half way down the grass avenue. The left leads to the rose garden, and the right to a terracotta ornament, a bust placed on an ornately decorated plinth with a hedge standing behind it. You have to turn left or right and then you suddenly find yourself in the garden with the borders, which seems especially spacious. In this way surprise is built into the approach to the flower garden. There are many ways to adapt this design to normal garden situations.

No way through into the garden In old gardens you often see a slightly sunken, stony garden with small rock plants before you step on to the grass and begin your walk along the borders. I sometimes put a pond in front of the terrace, so that you

Lavatera 'Barnsley' stands proudly beside Dianthus dalmatica.

45

have to walk round that. Then again, there could be a small formal garden, which prevents your walking straight through.

It sometimes happens that a client is more knowledgeable about plants than the landscape gardener, in which case the garden designer is asked to plan the shape and the client sets about filling in the plant borders him or herself.

This happened with a client from Zeeland Flanders, where I designed a large garden in stages. First I made an enclosed patio-like flower garden next to the living room and the kitchen, for sitting and eating in. After that came the design for the whole of the grounds with a large area on the east side of the house for trees, a border, and a large pond. On the south side there was a peep-hole into a neighbouring property that has long lines of poplars. A grass path led towards this view and there was a simple terrace beside the house. Borders in blue and purple tints flanked each side of the grass, with two yew hedges as background. The borders can easily be seen from the terrace, which is situated slightly higher. To give tranquillity to this terrace and to prevent too speedy a descent or walk along the borders, a "break" has been introduced in the form of a formal box garden. This is fascinating in the winter as well, when the borders are not, while emanating tranquillity and strength in its function as foreground.

Predominantly blue tints have been put in the borders, supplemented with purple. The type of ground here is white sand, which you would

White Lysimachia ephemerum *links the violet tints of* Lythrum *on the left and* Phlox *on the right, together making a strong group.*

not expect in clay-rich Zeeland Flanders. It is fascinating to see how everything grows so marvellously and blooms early here in wet seasons, whereas on the clay it is too wet. In the summer it soon gets too dry and too warm, so it has to be sprayed continually. Spraying borders is risky if they have roses in them. It is better to leave a dripping hose amongst the plants, which gives low moisture and prevents the flowers from getting slushy or rotting. Roses and phlox can be harmed by this, especially if they are sprayed regularly.

A pond as a break at a classical manor-house

A landscape gardener is seldom confronted with a completely fully grown garden which the clients have grown tired of. When this does happen it means great changes, and in the particular case with which I was confronted quite a large landscape garden had to be removed completely, including all sorts of trees, conifers, and shrubs. Fortunately I was not there when the trees were felled, though I am partly responsible because of my design for the new garden. My vision for a garden behind a stately manor-house was not a landscape lay-out but a strictly formal symmetrical garden design. That was what the clients wanted too. Where formerly shrubs had surrounded the garden, I designed a brick wall that I hoped would look splendid. In the centre of the garden, in the sight-line, I placed a summer-house as a high point of the new design. However, before you could reach this summer-house, the way through the garden had been designed according to a

A border of semi-wild flowers has been planted beside a long path. Malva *and* Liatris *bloom here with* Geranium *and* marguerite daisies, *which appear in the summer next to red poppies.*

Ton ter Linden lets the plants in his garden in Ruinen decide more or less for themselves how they behave after planting. Lythrum *is seen here next to red* Atriplex, *both vertical shapes.*

specific plan. It begins beside the house, with a spacious terrace of paving stones which match the formal house. After this grey terrace paths on both sides run into the garden at terrace level. The central part of the garden has been lowered by 30cm (12in) to create a "break", a sort of intermediate area, which gives intimacy and tranquillity to the large-seating terrace. You look over this lowered part towards a spacious, deep lawn with borders of perennials on both sides. In the sunken garden a rectangular pond has around it short-flowering roses and lavender. Behind this the lawn is subdivided into a front and spacious back section by means of a formal garden planted with box and short roses. The colours in the two borders (a combination of perennials and roses) are pink, purple, and blue, with lots of *Malva*, *Eupatorium*, and purple *Knautia*, the *Scabiosa*-like flower which I discovered in the castle garden at Walenburg and which I now use more and more as a permanent item in borders. It is an easy plant as long as it has enough room. The stems weave themselves amongst *Salvia*, *Phlox*, and the thistle-like *Eryngium*. A plant like this lends elegance, as does the perennial *Fuchsia*, the *F. magellanica*. Blue tints are provided by *Salvia*, *Nepeta*, and the blue-flowering lavender. Many roses have also been used.

The purely formal design is enlivened by a number of features which break things up. For instance, there are two sets of tables and chairs at

I could enjoy to my heart's content the colour combinations in this garden. Here you see Lythrum salicaria *'Morden's Pink' with* Polygonum amplexicaule *behind, which is deep carmine-purple and blooms endlessly in short spikes*

the ends of the paths which run down from the first large terrace. Both have been given a pergola to offset the asymmetry in the existing extensions. Wisteria, *Clematis montana,* and *Rosa* 'New Dawn' grow over these. One terrace is a wonderful sunny spot, while the terrace situated higher up is in the shade and has pots arranged on it. You could also have a statue on it or a large old-fashioned bird-cage with little white doves.

Against the back wall, on each side of the wooden summer-house, two water containers have been placed, above which water spouts from little pipes. This makes a pleasant sound if you are sitting in the summer-house, looking back into the garden. The wooden summer-house is splendidly fitted out with a Spanish table and Thai cane armchairs, which keep everything airy. When the whole white-painted garden-house was finished, it proved to me that you never stop learning, even as a designer.

The roof was made of grey tiles, and this combination seemed too white: it might have been better to have painted the garden-house mouse-grey. So my clients and I decided to grow ivy against it to reduce the white. The metamorphosis was unprecedented – from a luxuriant tree garden to an austere but still romantic, formal flower garden. Depth was achieved by the combination of violet, pink, and blue, which would not have been possible with yellow.

Rosa *'Gruss am Aachen' in the foreground forms the lead-up to a long pink and blue border. The idea of combining roses with perennials has long been established in England and is slowly spreading to other countries. Flowering can be considerably extended this way, and the colour combinations are a source of inspiration.*

Depth using delicate, receding colours

A few years ago I visited the garden of Crathes Castle in Scotland for the first time. The castle stands in a wood with old trees around it. All the floors are connected by two staircases and it has no side wings. This creates the narrow type of castle which is found particularly in Scotland. The ornamental gardens, or I should say the former kitchen gardens, are also typically Scottish. Once full of vegetables, they were of prime importance for survival in the remote places where these castles are often situated. This is why the kitchen gardens were surrounded by high walls – over which not even deer could jump. These enclosed spaces have often been made into ornamental gardens now that vegetables can be brought from the village shop close by. These castles are a source of delight for tourists and Scots alike, especially if flower gardens are added to them. Still, I in no way suspect Sir James and Lady Burnett of Leys of having arranged their garden for anyone other than themselves and a few friends.

The slightly sunken kitchen garden (whose walls you can easily look over from the castle) has been magically converted into an ornamental garden. And what a garden it is: it is generally regarded as one of the special perennial gardens of the world. There are different sections, such as a yellow garden and a spectacular white border which can be admired from both sides of a stone path as you walk into the garden. This border runs from wall to wall, across the narrower length of the rectangular kitchen garden. In the middle a cross path leads to other

Patricia van Roosmalen has created a delicate world of pink and blue tints in her garden in Rekum, in Belgium, in which the sturdy box shape forms a break. Gillenia, Erigeron, Campanula, and Geranium are good plants for helping to make a scene like this.

gardens and borders. The centre is formed by a *Prunus lusitanica*, which has been shaped into a gigantic globe on a stem. If you go left you come into a pink and blue garden.

The pink and blue garden of Crathes

Wooden supports have been placed around the garden, which has been planted completely in violet, pink, and blue tints. A large quantity of pink climbing roses grows over these supports. The *Geranium* varieties are violet, while the delphiniums, *Nepeta*, *Veronica*, and *Hyssopus* (the blue-flowering herb which is used too little in gardens) are all blue. There are also groups of grey-leafed plants, such as *Geranium pratense* 'Mrs Kendall Clark', *Veronica virginica* 'Alba', and *Macleaya cordata*. I was surprised to see the notorious rampant-growing *Macleaya* lending a slender emphasis amongst the perennials, which are slightly shorter. You have to turn the soil and weed conscientiously to keep these plants in check, which reproduce by means of underground shoots. But it is wonderful to see these grey stems with their large, lobeate, grey leaves rising up out of a rather flat border. I think *Macleaya* is also intended to act here as a counter-balance to the large groups of delphiniums, which are present in all sorts of colours, from light mauve to deep blue, and which are glorious when they are in flower. However, once flowering is over, there is little left. Hence the *Macleaya*, which masks the stems and the leaves of the delphiniums, or fills the gap when the stems have been cut down after

Lythrum salicaria *in the background with* Polygonum amplexicaule 'Roseum' *as foreground.*

Acanthus mollis *is the purple candle-like flower which stands out here in this splendid garden of borders.*

they have finished flowering. A subtle harmony is created by mixing numerous grey-leafed perennials with green-leafed roses and green-leafed perennials, the secret of which is planting in large groups. Large groups are interwoven with each other in wedges. There is a great deal of deep blue *Hyssopus, Delphinium, Salvia,* and *Veronica virginica,* which grows to a height of 1.6m (5ft 4in) and has light blue flowers.

My pink, blue, and purple Zeeland garden

A landscape gardener designs many gardens, which can be modern, romantic, formal, or historical in style. My basic principle is sometimes to look for a contrast, especially if the architecture is either very formal or very complicated, or else to look for harmony between the architecture and the garden. I chose the latter for my sixteenth-century farmstead, which is built of brick. The atmosphere of the building is medieval: the simple outline and the splendid tall pointed gable early Renaissance. For the longest elevation of the farm, in which two important rooms look out over what was once the kitchen garden, I designed a simple flower garden. Four beds with box hedges surround a square lawn. In the four large hook-shaped plant beds I put roses and blue-flowering perennials, as many as possible of those known in the sixteenth and seventeenth centuries so that some harmony with the architecture of the house was bound to arise of its own accord. For the roses I chose old-fashioned varieties, such as the apothecary's rose and *Rosa* 'Celsiana', which grows to a height of 2m (6ft) and has large pale

Scutellaria incana *stands in the dark foreground with blue* Salvia superba, *so the contrast with the pink plumes of the* Astilbe *is extra strong and convincing.*

pink flowers, *R.* 'Petite de Hollande', and *R. gallica* 'Versicolor', which is white with violet stripes in its petals. I also planted the purple-flowering *R.* 'Cardinal de Richelieu'. These bushes stand in the strip of ground which is joined directly to the lawn. I planted box globes in between and grey-leafed mint, *Mentha longifolia* 'Buddleia'. The problem with old-fashioned roses is that they bloom profusely, smell wonderful, but flower for a relatively short time. Therefore you need a lot of grey leaves with them, which I found in *Artemisia absinthium*, the grey-leafed wormwood which can grow to a good 1.5m (5ft) tall. I cut this silver-grey plant back once severely at the beginning of May so that it does not grow taller than 80cm (32in). I also planted *Cynara cardunculus*, also known as cardoon. This is the perennial artichoke, which makes new shoots every year. The leaves are silver-grey and pointed, and from their centre grows the large flower stem, which can grow 2m (6ft) tall in one season. These stand at the four corners of the large plant beds and are the tallest plants here with their purple-blue thistle-like flowers. I found more silver-grey in lavender, which appears to thrive wonderfully on the Zeeland clay. In the late spring, at the beginning or end of April (depending on the weather forecast), I cut back the lavender rigorously with hedge clippers, leaving a short, flat pancake. Then I cut off branches which are just about to shoot and just right for striking. If you plant them in the half-shade, possibly in the shade of a hedge or bush, 50 percent will survive. The grey foliage is

The white of Verbascum chaixii 'Album' forms the vertical lead-up to a large group of blue-violet flowers.

53

present all year round, and the blue flowers last from July into the autumn if you cut off the stems when they have finished flowering. An advantage of late spring pruning is that you can enjoy the broad grey clumps all winter long.

I always mix all sorts of herbs with roses to prevent disease. I plant lemon balm, pink and white mallow (*Malva moschata* and *M. m.* 'Alba'), rosemary, and even celery with roses – and successfully, as serious diseases like blight and mildew hardly ever occur. The effect of the herbs with the robust bush forms of the roses is like a wild planting: it looks very natural and takes away any stiffness from the roses. There can also be disappointments – only four of the eighty expensive Madonna lily bulbs came into flower. The rest were probably too dry in the summer or too wet in the spring, and hence shrivelled up. Who knows what will happen with these bulbs next year? I keep hoping for a miracle.

Pink and blue in the shade

In the shade I leave out grey, since grey in my opinion belongs in the sun and does not look as good in the shade. However, I shall mention later that there are possibilities for grey foliage.

Light colours belong in the shade, at least in nature. After all, insects need to be able to see the flowers in the dark, and all purple, blue, and certainly deep blue tints disappear in the shade. If we are to follow this

Campanula lactiflora spreads and takes on slightly different nuances: blue, pale blue, and almost white. It is the guiding principle of this border.

important lesson from nature, we must look for plants that have light pink and light blue flowers and that can stand full or half-shade.

My favourites

My greatest favourite is *Geranium endressii*, which stays in flower all summer. With *Geranium* I combine *Polygonum amplexicaule* 'Roseum', which has light lilac-pink flowers. The leaves are broad and elongated with an elegant sharp point. Long stems spread out upwards to support the long narrow flower spikes. The stems bend under the weight of the flowers, to create an elegant bouquet.

Less elegant in shape, but not in flowers, is the autumn anemone, of which there are many colour variations. *Anemone tomentosa* is often used and readily available. This is a good strong-flowering plant which does extremely well in the half-shade, and even much better on clay than in the fiercely drying sun, where it remains short. *A. t.* 'Albadura' grows to a height of 1.2m (4ft) and has light pink flowers: the outside is pink and the inside white. *A. t.* 'Robustissima' is bright pink, while the even more perfect *A. t.* 'Superba' has even richer pink flowers. My favourite is the white *A. hybrida* 'Honorine Jobert', but that does not belong in this summary of pink, unlike *A. hybrida* 'Queen Charlotte', which has half-full pure pink flowers and which remains shorter, at 90cm (36in). If you want a deeper colour amongst all the light pink choose *A. hybrida* 'Prince Henry', which is deep purple-red and half-full.

Purple and blue together in the garden of De Beukenhof in Oegstgeest. Anchusa *is blue,* cleome *purple or white.*

Left: Campanula lactiflora *'Loddon Anna' in the background is combined here with pink* Ceanothus *and white* Astrantia.

Following page: So many shades – mauve, pink, yellowish white, and yet a coherent whole.

55

Columbine also belongs among the shade plants, although it will quite happily stand in the open ground. It has a firm rosette of petals. *Aquilegia* 'Nora Barlow' is light violet with white spots on its petals, something unusual for collectors. I prefer *A*. 'Rosakönigin', which is pink with white and has beautiful foliage which stays splendid all summer. If the seeds, stems, and leaves are trimmed, fresh green foliage appears.

Astilbe has so many varieties that you can fill a garden with them. Whether it looks attractive depends on the plant combinations. There are numerous pink varieties which grow to medium height. *A*. 'Europa' is 50cm (20in) tall, and *A*. 'Peach Blossom' and *A*. 'Sprite' are both a salmony pink colour, which goes well with blue but not with violet. *A*. 'Rheinland', which grows to 50cm (20in), and *A*. 'Köln' are carmine pink. Some varieties have carmine tints which incline towards red, such as *A*. 'Vesuvius', 'Koblenz', and 'Granat'. They are not suitable for deep shade with light pink, but are fine in the half-shade. *A*. 'Betsy Cuperus' is a tall-growing thunbergii hybrid, which blooms light pink and is splendid in tall groups. All *Astilbe* varieties like shade which is not too dry, but also grow in the sun as long as they are in damp conditions. They are therefore ideal beside ditches, on the edge of river banks, and in tall groups.

It is wonderful to combine pink and blue with brighter tints. Ideal for

Distances are often blue; so if you do not have a view like this, use blue bushes and grey-leafed shrubs to match its effect, with pink-flowering perennials, annuals, and shrubs. Luckily they are good substitutes.

this is *Campanula lactiflora* 'Loddon Anna', which some people think of as pink, but I think of as blue. The "true" colour is somewhere in between, but the important thing is that the flowers provide brightness amongst darker colours. They go well with *Phlox, Chelone,* and autumn anemone, because their branches bend elegantly. Sometimes too elegantly, I have noticed, since the branches can become top heavy and, without support, you see only the bottom of the flowers. Therefore you must put them amongst supporting plants or tie them up. Supporting rings can solve this problem, though even this does not help if the branches spread out in the half-shade and become very long and slack.

I often cut out the tops when the stems grow so that they are forced to spread their branches out widely. Do this with half the stems and the bushy plants will flower in two sections. If, for instance, you have five plants, the three in the foreground can be cut down and you can let the two in the background grow taller.

Eupatorium purpureum *makes a very tall perennial with very upright branches. Flowering begins in the second half of the summer.*

Chelone obliqua has strong straight stalks, which do not suffer from the damp after flowering and stay upright for the whole winter. The foliage is a nondescript green and elongated, but the flowers are special: they form a cap on top of a basin-shaped lower flower in pink, purple, and violet tints. These plants are very suitable for large groups or as a streamer through other plants because they give sturdiness. Cut

Polygonum amplexicaule *is purple-crimson in colour. It is a strong plant which does not like ground that is too dry, and it can cope admirably with half-shade.*

out the heads after flowering and you will get a second flowering. This is an ideal flower for cutting.

Delphinium does not belong in the shade, and yet where is *D.* 'Astolat' more splendid than in the half-shade with its pink flowers and its black centre? Delphiniums cannot stand really deep shade, where they become straggly and fall over. *D.* 'King Arthur', another *Pacific Giant* hybrid, has a white centre in the middle of violet-coloured flowers, which means that it also looks splendid in the half-shade.

Dicentra has many varieties which are suitable for half-shade and are even quite happy in heavy shade. *D. eximea*, which has pink flowers and fresh green foliage, fits into this colour spectrum. *D. eximea* 'Boothman's Variety' is light pink, as is *D. formosa* 'Bountiful' which is a slightly deeper pink and has excellent grey foliage. This is a delight to the eye both before and after flowering because of its fine foliage. The leaves of the different kinds and varieties are fine and fernlike, some-times with a shimmer of blue. If you plant the front of the border with a combination of different shade-loving plants, the result is delicate and refined.

Equally refined is *Epimedium*, a foliage plant with fine leaves which always consist of two small leaves per stem: the bottom is wide and the top pointed. The flowers are small and delicate, in white, yellow, pink, and purple. The pink-flowering *Epimedium rubrum* is interesting.

Anemone tomentosa *in the mixed border of Powis Castle, Hertfordshire. Warm red-leafed and blue-flowering shrubs are combined with pink autumn anemones.*

E. *youngianum* 'Roseum' has lilac-pink flowers in early spring. *Filipendula* is also known as spirea and does in fact look rather like *Spiraea:* it has a plume-like way of flowering in various colours. *F. purpurea* has purple flowers and *F. p.* 'Elegans' carmine. *F. rubra* 'Venusta Magnifica' is carmine to red, while *F. r.* 'Venusta' is dark pink. *Filipendula* always does well in half-shade, where it blooms for longer. In full sun it is often a short-lived joy because the flowers wilt so quickly. The two latter varieties are 1.6m (5ft 6in) tall, the two former 60cm (24in). *Filipendula* is elegant as the background of a border or as a single plant in a shorter group. The foliage is beautifully shaped: slightly protracted with lobes. The pink tints in particular look bright in the half-shade if they are combined with the slightly purple *Polygonum amplexicaule,* which is somewhat darker.

Geranium is possibly the genus with the most varieties, and many of its sports have violet, pink, lilac, blue, or white flowers. Of the pink-flowering varieties, *G. endressii* is light lilac-pink and it blooms for a long time. I have had varying success with cutting off all the foliage and flower stems after the first flowering. Many people maintain that a second flowering will then follow, but I am by no means always successful so sometimes a bare patch is visible. Do this in a reasonably wet, early summer, and best of all just before you go on holiday. Then there will be some fresh leaves by the time you come back and the second flowering will follow. Otherwise, leave the stems alone and they will

In this peaceful, grand formal lay-out pink roses are combined with lady's mantle in the borders, thus introducing delicate colours which are, nevertheless, powerful.

keep producing some flowers. *G. e.* 'Wargrave Pink' is slightly more brick-red – a rather more difficult colour, which, however, looks attractive with deep purple tints. *G. clarkei*, of which *G. c.* 'Kashmir White' is the best known, has possibly the most beautiful foliage. Unfortunately it does not bloom for long, but the foliage compensates well for this. *G. c.* 'Kashmir Pink' has pink flowers and 'Kashmir Purple' violet flowers. *G. macrorrhizum* 'Spessart' quickly spreads out into a large group, with strong spicy leaves and a single profuse flowering. This ground-cover plant feels at home in the half-shade and remains fresh green there. In the bright sun and in dry conditions the leaves go rather red. *G. macrorrhizum* 'Album' is white with pink. *G. maculatum* 'Chatto's Form' grows to a height of 60cm (24in) and has pink-lilac flowers. For lazy gardeners there is *G. nodosum*, which blooms light purple-blue with little flowers which last for ages. Its foliage is fresh green. An advantage, or sometimes a disadvantage, is the fact that it spreads so much, which makes this *Geranium* either a nuisance or a relief. It is happy in deep shade. *G. phaeum* blooms naturally almost black-purple and grows to 80cm (32in) tall, and the variety 'Album' is white. Cut it back after flowering, then beautiful new foliage will appear. The *G. sanguineum* varieties (of which the 'Splendens' has pink flowers that are slightly darker veined and only grow to a height of 20cm [8in]), form a magnificent pink group. *G. s.* 'Jubilee Pink' is magenta pink, while *G. s.* 'Shepherd's Warning' is darker and

Dame's violet, (H. matronalis) in a large group with a lower group in front of Corydalis Ochroleura, which remains creamy white

redder. *G. s. striatum* is evenly pink and 25cm (10in) tall. This group is ideal in the foreground or amongst roses, for example, and is always powerful ground cover. You can put *G. pratense* 'Plenum Violaceum' with these, which is violet-blue and grows to 80cm (32in), and also *G. pratense* 'Silver Queen'. These plants can be used in all sorts of ways. I have planted *G. phaeum* and cut it almost to the ground after flowering. I also do this with the wild *G. pratense*, which grows beside Italian roads and has deep blue flowers. *G. endressii* is best left undisturbed, unless it is sufficiently warm and damp when the first flowering stops, in which case this can also be cut back.

For preference, choose varieties with attractive leaves that do not go brown after flowering, such as *endressii* and *clarkei*. *G. clarkei* has the most attractive foliage. Mix *Geranium* amongst stiff phlox, autumn anemones, and lungwort, which blooms in the spring. The modest flowers usually bloom for a long time and can brighten up darker plants.

Helleborus, the hellebore, is admired everywhere because of the moment at which it starts to flower: the flowers appear immediately after the frost and often as soon as the last night frost is over, and they can then bloom for a month or two. Many varieties have green or white flowers. *H. orientalis* blooms in mixed forms of white, pink, or purple. If you definitely want pink, buy flowering plants. *H. orientalis* 'Buck-

When making combinations you must pay attention not only to the colour, but also to the shape of the flowers. Here the round globes of Echinops *provide a lovely colour with the pink shape of* Campanula lactiflora *in front.*

shaw Hybrids' also blooms in these tints. *H. purpuruscens* (syn. *H. atrorubens*) blooms deep purple. Combine the green-flowering *H. corsicus* and *H. foetidus* with the pink and purple flowering varieties, or put them separately in groups. Combine them with short *Geranium* varieties, such as *G. clarkei* 'Kashmir White' which hangs its splendid foliage over the plants that have finished flowering. Alternatively, plant ferns amongst them, which spread their leaves over the plants which are often not so splendid in summer. Make sure you have some diversion tactics, especially with *Helleborus foetidus*, which has ugly, brown, dried-out flowers and seeds. You must leave these, however, as you will get seedlings from them if the ground is rich enough in humus. Neat gardeners, on the other hand, remove the dried-out flowers and enjoy the young shoots which suddenly appear. These combine beautifully with *Polygonum amplexicaule* 'Roseum', which hangs its stems over the *Helleborus*.

Flowering hosta usually does not appeal to me, but the flowers can be magnificent in a shady spot. The blue medium-sized leaves of *Hosta tokudama* 'Hadspen Blue' are crowned with lilac flowers. The foliage of *H. tardiana* 'Halcyon', which stays slightly smaller, growing to a height of 40cm (16in), has the same really bright blue colour. The flowers are dark pink-violet. *H.* 'Krossa Regal', which produces 1.2m (4ft) tall flower stems, is lilac-pink. *H. sieboldiana* 'Frances Williams' has the most striking foliage; it has pale lilac flowers and yellow edges

The kitchen-cum-cutting garden at Rhulenhof, where purple Phlox *are combined with hollyhocks,* Eupatorium, *goldenrod, and beans and tomatoes. This is right for a farm which also has some very refined flower gardens.*

to its enormous blue leaves. My two favourites are *H. crispula*, with its white edge and lilac flowers, and *H. fortunei* 'Aureomarginata', which has yellow-edged leaves. *Hosta* is a decorative foliage plant in the shade or half-shade which, as long as it is blue or yellow, helps to brighten darker plants.

Hemerocallis, the day lily, has narrow, elongated leaves and the plants are bushy with stems about 60cm (24in) tall, on which bell-shaped flowers appear. The most prevalent colours of this genus are yellow, browny yellow, and orange. There are also, however, apricot-coloured and red to browny-red varieties, and I once saw a purply-pink variety. The browny-red dark day lilies are splendid with pink tints.

Hyssopus or hyssop is one of the best flowering herbs I know. The spike-shaped blooms are like a cross between lavender and sage; they have a 15cm (6in) long stem with little deep blue flowers. Cut the plants back after flowering. Fortunately there are pink and white varieties too, otherwise they would not be mentioned here. *H. officinalis* 'Ruber' has pink flowers, grows only in the sun or light shade, and bushes out again every year.

Iris likes sun but can stand very light shade, so plant *I.* 'Rose Queen' in light shade; its large, elegant, mauve-pink flowers will brighten things up. The *I. germanica* hybrid 'Susan Bliss' also has pink flowers, while the *I. g.* hybrid 'Mrs Horace Darwin' is white with pink veins.

Ornamental onions with laburnum, the famous combination at Barnsley House, Gloucestershire, where you can even walk amongst the laburnum because the bushes are trained over arches.

Lamium is really a shade-loving plant, although many kinds and varieties do well in the sun too. *L. maculatum* 'Beacon Silver', which grows no taller than 20cm (8in), is true pink and has remarkable light green leaves, which have the appearance of silver-green.

L. m. 'Roseum' has numerous largish pink flowers, which also, however, reach a height of only 30cm (12in). A second pink-flowering herb is one of the versions of marjoram or oregano, *Origanum.* One of these has small, gold, variegated leaves and lilac-pink flowers. It is called *O. vulgare* 'Aureum'. A variety similar to this, *O. v.* Kempenhof', was found in a garden in Domburg, Zeeland, and has been named after the garden owned by Mrs Van Bennekom. It is lilac-pink with green foliage, and is 50cm (20in) tall. Both are suitable for half shade.

Completely unexpectedly, one now sees *Petasites,* or large butterbur, used as a perennial in gardens. It behaves like an untameable wild plant. This is why it is best "penned" between corrugated sheets of hard plastic or in masonry bins with a few holes in the bottom if necessary. This is not absolutely necessary, however, because they do not like to be too dry: half-shade or a damp spot is ideal. *P. hybridus* has pink flowers in the very early spring, and is naturally by marshy watersides. The flowers appear first, as a cluster on short stems, and only after they have finished blooming do the large, round leaves appear on long stems. *P. albus* has white flowers and *P. fragrans* pinky white.

A pink Phlox paniculata *hybrid stands next to a white form of* Veronica virginica, *which is approximately the same height.*

Moisture is essential, because they cannot stand dry shade. *P. fragrans* grows to a height of 25-30cm (10-12in).

An unfailing source of joy is *Phlox,* nearly all varieties of which thrive in half-shade.

Two pink *paniculata* hybrids are 'Elisabeth Arden,' which is pink with a light red centre (eye), and 'Evenlide,' which is purple-pink with a trace of mauve. Both are 1m (3ft) tall. The 'Mies Copijn' is a Dutch discovery and is a magnificent deep pink, as is 'Rijnstroom', also of Dutch origin. 'Flamingo' is a gentle pink, 'Lavendelwolke' mauve-pink, 'Rosa' pastel pink, and 'Rosa Spier' soft pink. In short, sufficient choice for half-shade! The *Phlox subulata* varieties, such as *P. s.* 'Marjorie', which has purple-pink flowers, and *P. s.* 'Moerheimii', which has pink flowers with a dark pink eye, remain short.

Platycodon has remarkable, slightly bell-shaped flowers, the petals of which are so bent towards each other when in bud that they create an elongated angular box. In Japan you see this plant in the wild in temple gardens. There is also a variety which can stand half-shade, *P. grandiflorum* 'Shell Pink'. The height of this is 40-50cm (16-20in) and it is usually grown for its flowers only.

A plant which we have had in our gardens since the Middle Ages is Jacob's ladder, *Polemonium caeruleum,* which is evenly blue. *P. carneum,* however, has pink flowers and is suitable for half-shade.

Pink and yellow do not always go together, especially if neither is of a soft tint. The beautiful grey wall and the light grey ornament here neutralize the yellow, so that the combination with pink is made possible.

65

Cut off the stems after flowering because they turn an ugly brown. Also, you will then prevent seedlings, which are very numerous!

Polygonum is also known as knotweed – I imagine because of the many little flowers which form spikes. *P. bistorta* is called snakeweed and has large oval leaves, above which long stems with pink to light pink spikes appear. It often blooms twice and loves damp situations. *P. amplexicaule* has almost been superseded by *P. a.* 'Roseum', which is certainly the most interesting amongst all these pink shade plants. It blooms from mid-July into the autumn, without a break. I would keep the height to about 1m (3ft). The plant likes to be not too dry and in half-shade. Its foliage will then stay fresh green.

Completely different from *Polygonum*, which is so delightful in the summer and autumn and which I would like to put in every garden, are the *Primula* varieties which are so spectacular in the spring. In the summer you only get a few leaves or the plant is completely dried out, so you must combine with them plants which grow wide, such as *Brunnera*, lungwort, or bush hortensias. *Primula juliae* remains short and has several pink-flowering varieties, such as 'Liz Green', which is deep pink, 'Groenekan', which is lilac, and the 'Primrose Guinever', which has soft pink flowers.

A garden without primroses that bloom so early, is incomplete, but unfortunately the colours are often bright and unnatural. The pink

This long, double border gives an impression of depth because many of the plants in the front row beside the narrow path have a rather upright way of growing and flowering.

varieties are splendid, so put them underneath shrubs and amongst perennials where they act as pink forerunners.

Rodgersia has characteristically beautiful leaves. They are sharply in-cised, like the leaves of a chestnut (Aesculus); this pattern is known as hand-shaped. The chestnut-like leaves of *R. aesculifolia* are embellish-ed with a splendid pink plume which sticks out above the leaves. The little flowers are whitish in colour. A true pink-flowering variety is *R. pinnata* 'Superba' with astilbe-like flower plumes. *R. henrici* also has pinky-red flower plumes, which grow very tall, 1.2m (4ft). All rodgersias like shade, and even deep shadow is no problem.

Pulmonaria forms an interesting combination with rodgersia, and many of its varieties are adorned with fascinating leaf shapes and colours. For instance, for years I have used *P. saccharata* 'Mrs Moon', which has pink flowers in tints which incline towards a really pale pink. I also like it because of its leaf shape and because of the light decorative flecks on its leaves, which look bright in the dark. The wild *P. angustifolia,* which has sky-blue flowers and the disadvantage of mildew forming on its long green leaves, does not have this flecked pattern. The *P. longifolia* varieties are true collectors' plants, which introduce into the garden a unique shape with their narrow elongated leaves. *P. longifolia* 'Dordogne' has violet-blue flowers. *P. saccharata* 'Argentea' has yellow flecks, and *P.s.* 'Margery Fish', named after the owner of the splendid garden at East Lambrook Manor, are pink with

Pale Campanula lactiflora *is combined with* Artemisia *'Schwefellicht' and, in the foreground, and as a contrast, a* Salvia *which has finished flowering still has some colour to offer.*

blue. For optimum effect put them in a group or in a straight line beside a path so that the leaves grow over the edge. If there is a grass path, plant them a little way from the edge so that the leaves are not destroyed when it is mown. The short *Viola cornuta* 'Victoria Cawthorne', which grows to a height of 20cm (8in), is then a good as foreground, as is *Geranium sanguineum* 'Violet'. Under bushes and preferably pruned into stem shapes, plant large separate groups of different varieties of *Pulmonaria*. Naturally, you would also want to introduce the magnificent blue-flowering varieties. Consider too the bright white-edged leaves of *Brunnera macrophylla* 'Variegata'. If you have a small garden or a small section of a large garden with shortish plants, you can plant *Pulmonaria* as a single specimen amongst *Vinca* (with its variegated leaves) and wild strawberries, or above *Artemisia schmidtii*.

Saxifraga is mostly a short plant with a rather old-fashioned aura. However, it really should be rediscovered. Our grandparents were mad about it, but now . . . And yet, *S. paniculata* (with its white-edged petals which stand in rosettes) is a beauty, particularly in the half-shade with its slender pink flowers above. It is certainly rather strange. A well-known apparition is *Symphytum*, comfrey, which occurs beside ditches in purple, white, and pink. If you can offer half-shade which is not too dry, you can plant *S. uplandicum* 'Variegatum' with its creamy yellow edges along elongated leaves.

Churchill was a fervent garden lover who also liked to take up a paintbrush. His yellow border is a treat with pink-violet accents here and there to offset too much of one colour.

A   ornament as eye-catcher to create depth
in the long perennial garden

B   grass path

C   white farmhouse with exhibition area for
ornaments

1   *Echinops bannaticus* 'Taplow Blue'

2   *Centaurea montana*

3   *Aster* 'Plenty'

4   *Rosa* 'Tapis Volant'

5   *Rosa* 'Fru Dagmar Hastrup'

6   *Rosa* 'Pernille Poulsen'

7   *Agastache foeniculum*

8   *Geranium endressii*

9   *Artemisia arborescens* 'Powis Castle'

10 *Iris sibirica*

11 **Phlox paniculata hybrid**
'Lavandelwolke'

12 *Stachys grandiflora*

13 *Eupatorium purpureum*

14 *Delphinium* 'Lady May'

15 *Rosa* 'Complicata'

16 *Rosa* 'Pearl Drift'

17 *Rosa* 'Betty Prior'

18 *Lavandula angustifolia* 'Munstead'

19 *Pulsatilla vulgaris*

20 *Polemonium* 'Down Flight'

21 *Crambe cordifolia*

22 *Scabiosa caucasica*

23 *Buddleia alternifolia*

24 *Ilex crenata* 'Convexa'

25 *Chrysanthemum coccineum* hybrid

26 *Hosta sieboldiana* 'Elegans'

27 *Artemisia ludoviciana*

28 *Rosa* 'Marguerite Hilling'

29 *Chelone obliqua*

A garden in Sambeek

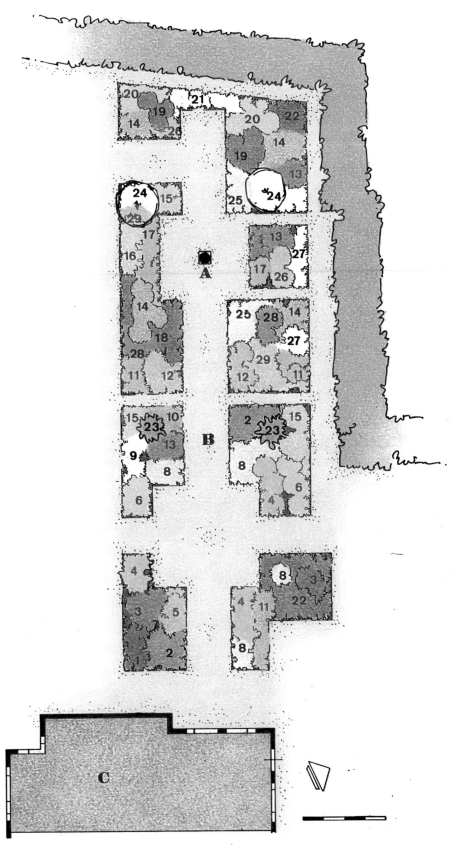

Decorative foliage

Plants which we grow for their flowers are, of course, marvellous, but unfortunately flowers do not last for ever. Hence leaf shapes are also of great importance - and leaves are what you look at for the longest.

The foliage's shape of the foliage can be an extra bonus, particularly when a plant has finished flowering. And, the fact that, in most cases, flowering unfortunately comes to an end quite quickly makes the shape of the foliage very important. Large leaf shapes or very precise incised, lobeate, unusually coloured, or marked smaller leaves can be very striking.

However, you must be careful with large leaves in small gardens as they will make the garden look smaller. On the other hand, very fine incised or other types of fine leaves will make your garden appear deeper. This is because when you look into the distance you no longer distinguish shape but structure. The leaves of *Petasites* are seen at a great distance as structure, while close up they appear as large leaves.

The same is true of *Symphytum, Crambe, Darmera,* and *Rudbeckia.* To make very subtle use of these leaves and thus create an illusion of depth, you must put large leaf shapes at the front of the garden and small ones at the back.

Large leaf shapes at the front, small ones at the back

In a small garden you can put *Hosta* at the front, and *Geranium, Phlox,* and autumn asters at the back to achieve depth. In a large garden you can combine *Gunnera* or *Darmera* (Peltiphyllum) at the front with *Phlomis, Brunnera,* and *Bergenia,* and put the fine-leafed species and varieties at the back. Many large-leafed plants like to be damp. *Gunnera,* the Brazilian marsh plant, which does so well in

Peltiphyllum peltatum *looks like butterbur but does not grow rampant. The foliage is lobeate and turns a beautiful red in the autumn. In the spring the plant has curtains of pink flowers on tall stems.*

European gardens, thrives only if you take the trouble to keep the ground damp and if you plant it in half-shade.

Poppies in a red border Wild poppies are often seen as spectacular undergrowth to olive trees or growing in fields that are ploughed in the autumn and then left alone. Anyone who has travelled in such countries as Italy, France, Austria, and Switzerland will be familiar with the many poppies that grow under fruit trees which are not properly maintained or sometimes under olive trees. Apparently, the ground is turned there only after the poppies have flowered and the seeds are ripe, and the result is an inevitable carpet of bright red poppies. This is what we are after when we sow wild red poppies, but we tend to forget that open ground and not an enclosed plant bed is the secret of success with poppies.

Cultivated poppies usually bloom once and abundantly and, as far as I know, no continuously blooming variety has been developed. So we must be content with one flowering period and large leaves afterwards. As long as they are planted correctly, poppies can contribute to a good planting design. Put poppies next to later-flowering plants such as globe thistle, *Echinops ritro*, or *Achillea*, both classic combinations (especially with *A. filipendulina* 'Cloth of Gold' and *A. f.* 'Parker's Variety'). Put lavender with them and blue-flowering *Salvia*, preferably continuous-flowering varieties, such as *S. nemorosa* 'Blauhügel,' which is 40cm (16in) tall, *S. n.* 'Tänzerin,' which is purple blue and

Ulmus carpinifolia 'Wredei,' the golden elm, has very striking leaves. They are curled and a magnificent golden yellow. I created an avenue of them here, with a wealth of yellow perennials around them.

73

Hosta crispula has a white border to its green leaves. It is a good plant for the shade, where it acquires its most splendid colours. Here you can see it with Matteuccia struthiopteris, *the ostrich feather fern, which also has great decorative value as a foliage plant*

90cm (36in) tall, or *S. n.* 'Wesuwe,' which is 60cm (24in) tall. You will then compensate, to some extent, for the sight of all the foliage of the orientale varieties. Red is the most familiar colour for poppies, and this is suitable for a cheerful garden or a blood-curdling red garden border! Red borders are slowly becoming more popular.

In England I have seen poppies in two famous gardens, one of which was Hidcote Manor Garden. Lawrence Johnston (an American brought up in Europe) bought a romantic old house in Gloucestershire that was in a rather remarkable location – the grounds run upwards behind the house and not downwards, as one normally sees. Apparently this was made into a garden only later, as initially sheep grazing in a meadow on an incline like this was quite attractive enough. However, a garden which slopes upwards brings problems – unless you have a good design on paper or in your head which was the case with this plant collector. By often looking out of his back windows, the solution came of its own accord. Directly behind the house three gardens had been laid out on more or less flat ground: a flower garden behind the house underneath a broad old Cedar of Lebanon was followed by a grass path with two pink-flowering borders containing a great deal of grey and some blue. Then there was a stone gateway with a wrought-iron gate, beyond which there was a round space: a circle of grass with a paved path around it so that the grass was not ruined in wet weather. Around this

Hosta leaves come in all sizes and there are all sorts of different colours too. Hosta fortunei 'Aureomarginata' *has green leaves with a golden yellow border.*

circle was a red beech hedge. After that, along the sight axis in the depth of the hollow, a red border had been made, which was crowned with a flight of steps with two Dutch pavilions full of Delft-blue tiles. This was followed by two clipped hornbeam blocks *(Carpinus betulus)*, to the left and right of the axis and finally brings the top of the hill. Here the sheep meadow slopes downwards, with old oaks as the surprising denouement.

When discussing red borders, people often complain that there are too many harsh colours. So red borders will never be really popular, which is a shame because, as with all colours, red occurs no more profusely than black, white, or blue. There are so many nuances of red that you must learn to deal with them as an artist would to create something fascinating. This idea first occurred to me at Hidcote Manor Garden. The secret here is the use of deep red, almost black-purple shrubs, which are planted in the background. I remember, for instance, the red hazel, *Corylus maxima* 'Purpurea', and the red *Berberis ottawensis* 'Superba', which grows to a height of 2m (6ft) and has deep red oval leaves. *Berberis thunbergii* 'Red Chief' also has purple-coloured leaves with steeply upright-growing branches that fan out elegantly. Other plants in the border were red roses, red Canna, red dahlias, *Geum*, and the annual purple cosmea. There was also a waving grass that I saw for the first time here and that has since become part of my garden

If you look at the leaves of lady's mantle, Alchemilla, *after dew or rain, you will discover a pearl! The greyish foliage is splendid. Cut everything back in July and you will have fresh leaves and a second flowering.*

language: *Miscanthus sinensis* 'Gracillimus'. *Dracaena* on tall stems with purple-brown leaves completed the picture with its fine, moving foliage. All this created a rather Mediterranean atmosphere. There were also red poppies at the front of the border at Hidcote, the *orientale* varieties such as red 'Goliath', which grows 1m (3ft) tall, deep orange 'Marcus Perry', and the 80cm (32in) tall 'Indian Chief', which has mahogany-coloured, and therefore deeper red, flowers. Bear in mind that all poppies grow rampant and are difficult to get rid of. So think twice before you plant them and then take the plunge with these very strong, permanent plants.

If you do not like red you will find plenty of delicate colours. Of the poppies in delicate colours *Papaver orientale* 'Mrs Perry', which flowers in a very fine tint of salmon pink, is very popular. *P. o.* 'Salmon Glow' is more salmony-orange, while *P. o.* 'Wendekind' is satin pink.

If you have a small garden you will have enough with just one *P. orientale*. Put plenty of grey and blue around it, or otherwise keep to light colours for the rest of the border: *Lysimachia ephemerum* is a good neighbour at the back with its white candles of fine flowers on 1.5m (5ft) stems and its greyish foliage, and so is the white *Anemone hybrida* 'Honorine Jobert', which grows to the same height. Put *Gypsophila paniculata* in front and a *Crambe* next to it. You can put white-flowering *Iris germanica* here with its sword-shaped leaves, and some white fleabane, *Erigeron*, to give a wild effect. This will detract from the effect created when the poppies are pulled up after they have flowered.

Arranging a red border

Start by planting a few purple-leafed shrubs. Red-leafed *Cotinus coggyria* 'Rubrifolius' is a good plant to begin with; this bush grows to about 2m (6ft) tall. The fluffy blooms, which are often yellowish, are attractive and soon go a greeny colour and cover the whole plant. Trim a number of short red-leafed *Berberis thunbergii* 'Atropurpurea Nana' into round globes in the foreground and, if there is room, put an easily pruned red hazel next to them. This can grow to 3m (10ft) tall, but can also be trimmed into a flat shape. After this choose a few elegant plants, such as ornamental grasses, or a few red-flowering plants, preferably Polyantha roses.

The red *Papaver orientale* and *Lychnis chalcedonica*, *Maltese Cross*, go well here with, for example, the red-flowered *Sedum telephium*, 'Munstead Dark Red'. There are many bright red annuals, from geraniums *(Pelargonium)* to *Fuchsia* and red *Salvia*. There are also many deeper red tints, in particular *Cosmos atrosanguineus*, which has purple-red flowers in a small daisy form that appear bright red when they have just come out. There are plenty of *Monarda* varieties, such as *M.* 'Cambridge Scarlet', 'Adam', which is cherry red, and 'Mahogany', which is a vivid red, and all of which go on blooming for a long time and have long been familiar as permanent items in herb gardens.

Following page: The two shades - certainly when combined with the alternating shapes of the planting - make an exciting patch in the garden

Ornaments in the garden
Ornamental rhubarb

Rheum is at the top of my list of favourite easy foliage plants. Ornamental rhubarb blooms like normal rhubarb; it has a long stalk with a long, quite thick flower plume. *R. palmatum* has green, slightly purple-tinted leaves. *R. p. tanguticum* has red leaves when it shoots and after that it goes a greeny-red colour. Use *Rheum* on its own or in large groups if your garden is big enough. You need a great deal of room for a group, because the flower stems grow to 2m (6ft) tall and the leaves to 1-1.5m (3-5ft). These are good supporting leaf shapes with birches, hoary willows, and *Prunus.* In a small garden you could possibly have one specimen plant.

On the east and west sides of Vondel Park in Amsterdam there are some very fine mansions. I designed a garden for one of these. It is small compared with the richly embellished, romantic building, which dates from the end of the nineteenth century. The small garden could not compete with the building, so my solution was a centrally situated round pond in which the buildings' façade would be reflected. Seen from the house, this brings new excitement to the garden, not just because of the round mirror with its diameter of 5m (16ft) but also because of the varied planting around it. All sorts of "friendly" leaf shapes (*Brunnera, Aquilegia, Hosta crispula* (white border), *Iris sibirica, Thalictrum, and Alchemilla*) make a delicate carpet and give height. The sturdy shape of *Rheum* is the strong element here, which gives counterbalance to the pond and the façade. The large deeply

In large gardens it is a good idea to combine upright forms with an easily visible transition point now and then, which reveals the leaves and the stems of the taller groups.

Left:
Yellow flags look like swords coming out of the water. The Latin name is Iris pseudacorus.
If you like white striped leaves, choose I. p. 'Variegata'.

incised leaves appear early and remain hanging over the edge of the large pond until well into the autumn. Later a lamp-post was added with a very large crystal ball in cobalt blue, which gives a nice colour with *Iris sibirica*, *Brunnera* and the blue aquilegias.

Rodgersia *Rodgersia* is a delight for those who like large leaf shapes. Plant them in large groups under bushes beside water or in the shade of a wall, house, or fence.

There is a choice between incised leaves which are hand-shaped, or round leaves such as those of *Astilboides tabularis* (formerly classified with *Rodgersia*), which is fresh green in colour. Above these put broad, white flower plumes. *R. pinnata* has a bronze-coloured sheen over the leaves and pink flower plumes. *R. aesculifolia* has large, slightly curved leaves with cream flower plumes which can grow to a good 1.5m (5ft). *R. podophylla* 'Braunlaub' has brownish leaves and cream flowers and grows to 1.2m (4ft). Combine *Rodgersia* with more large leaf shapes and with a tranquil carpet of green underneath. *Vinca, Waldsteinia, Pachysandra terminalis, Galium,* and tongue ferns are all suitable as a tranquil background.

Plant green and white flecked *Pulmonaria* or bushy ornamental grasses such as *Miscanthus sinensis* 'Silberfeder' and *M. s.* 'Gracillimus' with them: the first is upright and the second bends elegantly outwards. The foliage of *Ligularia przewalskii* is also perfect because

This grey-leafed plant whose lemon-yellow flowers appear very early in the spring is called Euphorbia characias wulfenii.

it is very finely incised and the flowers are long and vertical. *Thalictrum* varieties are also good with *Rodgersia*, because they grow upright and slender and bloom with enchanting purple clusters of small flowers.

Romneya coulteri

Romneya coulteri is a half-shrub with splendid sea-green foliage. However, even more splendid is this peony's flower: white with a large yellow heart. This makes it a striking foliage and flowering plant, which looks beautiful with rue (*Artemisia*) and *Helianthemum* 'The Bride' (the grey-leafed ground-cover plant with the same flower colour combination but which is much smaller).

Rudbeckia

Rudbeckia is a good foliage plant which also has great flowering value. The large leaves are incised, so rather than being large, green, and floppy, they are more like long strips of green which hang over one another. The flowers are usually yellow and the long yellow petals sit beneath a blackish-brown conical heart.

There is also a purple *Rudbeckia* (which is called *Echinacea* these days) that has far less striking foliage but splendid flowers. *Rudbeckia fulgida* 'Goldsturm' can grow to 1m (3ft) tall, and *R. laciniata* 'Goldquelle' grows to the same height. *R.* 'Aurea' grows even taller, if possible, to 1.75m (5ft 9in). The blue-leafed *R. maxima* is an odd variety, which is planted for its foliage.

Iris is planted not just for its splendid leaves but also for its flowers. Before and after flowering, the sword shapes of the long leaves are magnificently frosted with grey.

80

Salvia argentea This is possibly the most striking plant in the border, together with *Cynara cardunculus* (the silver-grey perennial artichoke) and *Onopordum*, which can both grow to a height of 2-3m (6-10ft). If the greeny flower spikes are removed, there is a good chance that this biennial will become a permanent border inhabitant. *Salvia sclarea*, one of the mainstays of many borders, is slightly less silvery-haired. Unfortunately it is a biennial and the light mauve inflorescences only appear in the second year. The foliage is grey and light in colour, and its height is 80-100cm (32-3ft).

Smilacina *Smilacina racemosa* is sometimes called false Solomon's seal – a rather strange name since there is nothing false about this plant. Possibly the shape of the leaves, which resemble those of Solomon's seal, has caused the confusion. Broadly elongated fresh green leaves appear on either a straight or a slightly bent stem, with a cream-white flower plume above. It is well worth having in the shade, where it brightens the darkness.

Symphytum Comfrey has an almost irrepressible growing capacity: the elongated leaves grow so enormous that you sometimes have to apply the shears to allow fresh green young leaves to come out. *Symphytum caucasicum* is good ground cover for large areas, where the magnificent blue bells appear on top. *S. uplandicum* 'Variegatum' has variegated leaves

Packwood House, Warwickshire, has magnificent multi-coloured borders which deserve to be better known. Yellow with lilac, blue-mauve, and pink are united here in majestic borders. In this way a straight path becomes exciting because each step reveals a new picture.

81

with creamy-white borders, which are very striking in half-shade and deeper shade. It combines well with the yellow flowers of lady's mantle and, for example, *Kirengeshoma* and *Ligularia przewalskii*. The height is 70cm (28in) and the flower colour light lilac. To be honest, this combination is not unduly attractive but the foliage will make you completely forget this.

Polygonum *Polygonum* is one of the most surprising garden plants I know. The extended family includes the wildest climbing plants that can grow rampant over whole houses, and also subtle ground-cover plants. One of the subtle *Polygonum* varieties is *P.filiforme*, which has long red cord-thick inflorescences consisting of numerous small flowers. All *P. filiforme*, wherever they are growing, come from the garden of Walenburg Castle. Many cuttings were given to nurseries to give the plant a permanent place in Dutch gardens. It is one of the many plants from Walenburg that have become popular because of the clever way they were used there. This non-herbaceous *Polygonum* would have been completely overlooked had it not been planted in Walenburg next to *Rosa* 'Constance Spry' on each side of a stone bench over which a climbing rose hangs.

The large double-pink flower was cultivated by David Austin, who has now cultivated for us a whole series of continuous-flowering, and what

Goat's beard, aruncus dioicus, formerly also known as sylvestris, is a shade-cum-woodland plant. The flower plumes go from creamy white to brown, but the leaves are strong and feathered and remain in place.

The leaves of Acanthus mollis *were the inspiration for the Greeks when they decorated the capitals of their pillars.*

appear to be antique shrub roses. Snakeweed, *Polygonum bistorta,* is one of those wild plants which once came from abroad and are now so at home that they behave like wild plants in their new habitat. Above the broadly elongated leaves, which end in a point, can be seen the flower spikes, which rock on green stems in the wind. After flowering, cut away the flower stems and you will often get a second flowering. *P. bistorta* 'Latifolium' is pure pink and has 70cm (28in) tall inflorescences. *P.* 'Compactum' grows no taller than 40cm (16in). *Reynoutria japonica* (Polygonum cuspidatum) has large leaves and light white-pink flowers. This giant reaches a height of 1.75m (5ft 9in). The flower shapes look bright along the water's edge. All *Polygonum* species are inclined to spread healthily, so you must restrict their growth if your garden is small.

I have mentioned *P. amplexicaule* several times (which blooms purple-red and has elegant broadly elongated leaves) and *P. a.* 'Roseum'. There is also a white *P. a.* 'Album'. You can use *Polygonum* in borders or as a semi-wild plant. They can be mown but will still come back. In my experience a spot in the half-shade keeps the leaves looking nice for longer.

Pulmonaria

Pulmonaria sometimes has large leaves and sometimes small. *P. saccharata* 'Mrs Moon' is middle sized and is white flecked with lilac flowers. All *P. longifolia* varieties, such as 'Bertram Anderson'

Lupinus *has attractive hand-shaped leaves. Here you see the creamy-white* Lupinus polyphyllus *hybrid 'Obelmaiden', which goes silvery white.*

and 'Dordogne', are striking foliage plants, which owes more to the shape of their very long narrow leaves than to their size.

Telekia

Telekia has large elongated leaves, which are wide at the beginning and in the middle. This striking perennial plant has golden-yellow daisy-like flowers. It is 1.3m (4ft 3in) tall.

Verbascum

The large pointed leaves of *Verbascum* can be integrated into the general planting in two ways. I have planted *Malva* and *Geranium* species with it, which are also slightly pointed but more hand-shaped. You can create a great contrast if you plant *Iris germanica* hybrids (known as bearded iris) with it. You will achieve a vertical contrast with the horizontal broadly elongated *Verbascum* leaves, and the grey colours also go together well. The finely incised leaves of *Artemisia schmidtiana* – which could hardly be dissected further – form a refined grey blanket, above which the *Verbascum* leaves emerge. Most cultivated mulleins have green leaves that are almost always elongated. A popular one is *Verbascum chaixii* 'Album', the white mullein, which has green leaves and grows to a height of 1.2m (4ft). The apricot-coloured *V.* 'Cotswold Queen' and the soft yellow 'Gainsborough' are the same height. 'Pink Domino' is pink and 90cm (36in) tall, while 'Royal Highland' is again apricot-coloured. The wild *Verbascum thapsus* is light yellow and looks good with its fluffy-grey foliage. This

Geranium psilostemon *has dark violet flowers with a black heart. Here it is combined with yellow mullein, which is tall and vertical, and short* Santolina.

Verbena hastata *is purple-blue and deserves to be planted more often.*

is still my favourite, even though the other new varieties have more refined colours. Yellow is the basic colour of this genus, which occurs in the wild in dry sandy spots. Mullein seems to be at home on sandy ground, somewhere in the neighbourhood of water. In such a spot they can come up again every year in their thousands, completely covering the ground with a beautiful yellow. Also yellow are *V.* 'Albian', which has a bronze-coloured heart and 1.5m (5ft) tall flower stems, and *V.* 'Cotswold Gem', which stays slightly shorter and has bronze-yellow flowers with violet-purple hearts. *V.* densiflorum is dark yellow with a violet-purple heart, while 'Yellow Princess' is vivid yellow. All are 1.5m (5ft) tall. In short, you can make powerful groups of *Verbascum*, which flower continuously. For extra flowering, remove the stem from the plant when it has finished flowering, otherwise flowering come to an end much sooner. After the last flowering, stop cutting away the mulleins to keep the dried vertical shapes as winter decoration in the garden.

Kniphofia *Kniphofia,* red hot poker, is a remarkable plant, loathed by many but quite unjustly. However, you soon tire of seeing orange African marigolds, pink geraniums, and a clump of the rather strange red hot poker flowers in front gardens. This is a shame, because good combinations are possible, particularly in a red-orange border where they form a marvellous group with orange *Alstroemeria aurantiaca* 'Orange King',

Red roses lend themselves well to combinations in an orange-red border.

Helenium 'Moerheim Beauty', and the bright orange *Hemerocallis* 'Orangeman'. If you have a lot of the small fine leaves of *Phlox*, *Geranium*, and *Alstroemeria*, the slightly arched hanging leaves of *Kniphofia* can provide a good strong shape which gives rhythm and breaks up too much haziness. If there are more long leaves, such as those of *Hemerocallis,* then you must choose: either make a composition of long leaves with the round leaf shapes of *Ligularia* and white-flowering *Bergenia*, or hide the *Kniphofia* leaves behind other foliage of, for example, *Salvia*, *Artemisia*, roses, or ornamental grasses. This can be done without problem so the rather untidy, bushy leaves need not be a reason for banning this plant from the garden. There are also other colours apart from the orange-red varieties, such as *K. pfitzeri* (coral red), *K. praecox* (bright red), *K.* 'Alcazar' (pomegranate red), *K.* 'Earliest of All' (orange with yellow), *K.* 'Jonkheer van Tets' (orange), and *K.* 'Royal Standard' (yellow with orange). *K. caulescens*, particularly in the variety 'Maid of Orleans', has a rare lemon colour.

Ligularia dentata 'Desdemona' has deep yellow flowers and brownish-green foliage. It is a good supporting plant in a multi-coloured garden with red, blue, and white tints.

The iris - a plant to collect

The well-known flower arranger and teacher, Andrea van Rijckegem, has hidden herself away in an ordinary little street of exquisite houses. And who would expect such a surprising atmosphere behind this innocent façade? The house is full of objects, there are classrooms, sales-rooms for vases and Japanese bowls for Ikebana, and right behind the house there is a large green lawn with old fruit trees, where a

French table with bistro chairs waits for a "lunch à la campagne" to be served or a cool summer drink. An attractive small barn shuts off one side of the garden which is full of red geraniums that bloom profusely. Everything here speaks of rustic simplicity and tranquillity. A dark wall is visible in the distance, with some wild rose branches hanging over it. Behind this wall is hidden the flower garden, which has long beds containing all the flowers and shrubs needed for flower arranging and inspiration. For there is much coming and going in the classrooms of ladies and gentlemen who learn here how to deal with flowers in European or Japanese style. However, most of the flowers in the garden are left where they are, as a source of inspiration for the students and for Andrea herself. In a yellow garden with *Phlomis*, yellow day lily, and creeping jenny, I saw for the first time the creeping indigenous plant that is recorded as *Lysimachia nummularia* – the lemon-yellow red hot poker. It stood brightly beside large bushes of the delicate blue *Hydrangea macrophylla* 'Mariesii Perfecta', which has grey-blue pseudo-flowers and light real flowers that form the large centre of the inflorescence which is shaped like pin-pricks. This made a lasting impression on me, because it must have been five years ago since I last saw it and photographed it as a source of inspiration.

Lemon yellow with blue can be the theme of a garden, in which case *Kniphofia* suddenly becomes important. Combine this with *Cephalaria gigantea* or *Cephalaria tchihatchewii*, both of which grow to a height

Artemisia ludoviciana *'Silver Queen' stands in the middle, and on the left is* Stachys byzantium *with slightly different colours that combine subtly with the roses.*

of 2m (6ft). They bear lemon-yellow scabiosa-shaped flowers on long, slender stems and are miracles of elegance and ornamentation. Yellow pansies, *Achillea ptarmica*, and *A. taygetea* also fit in well here, as does *A. irengeshoma,* so long as it is in the shade of the bushy *Cephalaria.*

Iris is a flower of antiquity, which is, however, still the favourite of many present-day garden lovers. One example of lovers of the iris is Jan de la Hayze, who has devoted himself to collecting and studying this flower in his town garden in Middelburg –one of the most beautiful gardens in The Netherlands. Much can be learned from this collector' s garden.

A grass path that is attractive in both the winter and the summer has a terrace at one end and a little stone pillar with a yew globe pruned above it at the other. White hortensias and ferns surround it. Beside the grass path, broad spacious plant beds are reserved for the collection, and a yew hedge closes off these beds. A globe ornament forms the introduction to the iris garden. Jan de la Hayze devotes himself as much as possible to collecting blue tints, with a few other tints as well. In flower, the garden is a true spectacle of blue. Afterwards, the ornaments and the composition as a whole take over from the sword-shaped leaves which, though admittedly splendid in themselves, can sometimes go rather yellowy.

Astrantia can be combined with many other flower colours and shapes because of its simplicity.

This long border is different every year because of the freedom given to the seeding plants. The background is formed by Taxus media *'Hicksii'.*

I have often been confronted with plants that could not be persuaded to flower and just, as often, I have have been confronted with ugly colour combinations. But when you see a great deal, the good examples remain and you forget the rest. Therefore I am still quietly convinced by foliage that introduces a vertical play of lines in the whirl of round-leafed perennials and plants with incised leaves. And if the flower goes well with the perennials or roses, this is a great gain. A feeling for colour is important in making the correct choice, and so is knowledge of the right sort of ground (limy), and the position for the thick rhizome on the ground (not *underneath*). Sun is also a requirement and ground which is not too wet; dry conditions appear not to be harmful to iris. Even so, it is important to make a distinction between the different varieties. There are moisture-lovers, such as *Iris sibirica* varieties and *I. kaempferi* varieties, and those which like dry conditions, such as *I. germanica* hybrids.

This effect of blue cloudy flowers can be achieved with either Geranium 'Johnson's Blue' or with autumn asters. The aster 'Rudolph Goethe' is lavender blue and grows to a height of 60cm (24in), so this can be your autumn-flowering plant. In the middle is a red currant.

Iris germanica hybrids

I knew this plant from old books about herbs, which described how the roots were ground finely and the powder used in therapeutic recipes. *I. germanica* does not come from Germany but from dry Mediterranean areas, where the iris always occurs on porous stony ground and in rocky situations, beside verges which are well drained, but mostly on the walls of farmhouses. The spread-out rhizomes lie on the walls with soil between them and the wall. Apparently, this is their favourite

89

Festuca glauca is combined here with the equally grey bushes Salix *and* Pyrus salicifolia *in an unexpected pond garden*

growing situation. So you can use pieces of brick or other broken stone as coarse gravel to achieve good drainage on sites where iris is to be planted, and also to raise the site slightly above its surroundings, again for good drainage.

If it is not possible to do this, lay drainage under the grass or stone path which runs beside the irises. Remember, too much water is fatal to them.

I. germanica was the symbol of the gods and the worldly kings who wished to identify themselves with the gods. This is why the 'Fleur de Lys' became the symbol of the French royal house. The three pointed petals of the wild *Iris germanica* is the image that was developed into the familiar regal shape and which is reproduced on, amongst other things, silk, porcelain, and wood.

Apart from the wild *I. germanica*, many descendants have been cultivated over the centuries. Many irises are blue, including varieties such as the *I. g.* hybrid 'Alcazar' (lavender blue), the *I. g.* hybrid 'Corrida' (soft blue), and the *I. g.* hybrid 'Empress of India' (light blue). White varieties include the *I. g.* hybrids 'White Knight' and 'White City' (white with a touch of light blue). The *I. g.* hybrid 'Californian Gold' is golden yellow and one of the many golden species and varieties which have been cultivated. The *I. g.* hybrid 'Helga' is lemon-yellow and 'Amber' again has a golden yellow tint. There are bronze-coloured and violet-

This border (in which tall Lythrum salicaria *'Morden's Pink' gives a violet colour accent) is hazy, like a wild strip of meadow flowers. In front are grey* Artemisia *and yellow lady's mantle, which are both hazy in colour.*

red varieties, since with Iris germanica hybrids you are not dealing with just a single colour but with the colour of the upright, upward-facing petals, which are called "standards," and the hanging petals, known as "falls", which are sometimes of a different colour. The 'Ambassador', for instance, has bronze-violet standards and deep violet falls. So they combine well with *Geranium psilostemon, G. sanguineum,* and with the pale yellow of *Cephalaria, Alchemilla,* and *Achillea taygetea.*

The *I. g.* hybrid 'Lent A. Williamson' has purple-violet standards, while the falls are violet, and 'Salonique' has creamy-yellow standards and dark violet falls. These colours can be integrated into a border with soft greys, violets, and pale yellows. For lilac garden plants, such as autumn anemones and phlox, there is the *I. g.* hybrid 'Mrs Horace Darwin', which is white with lilac veins in its petals. In short, if you once fall in love with irises, you will usually remain in love with them.

In Florence you can choose Near the Piazza Michelangelo in Florence (the large square right near the centre of town with a splendid view over the city, the River Arno, and the surroundings), you can visit an annual iris garden. I usually go there in May and each time I write down the names of the irises with the most subtle or daring colours. Immaculate ladies, volunteers from the Italian iris associations, offer in a very friendly manner all the information you want about the irises, which are planted on a slope in

Blue Salvia nemorosa *sweeps through a field of* Achillea *like a wave of blue, with a large* Hosta *in the foreground. This is large-scale gardening for which you need space.*

Iris pumila,
the short
bearded iris

an olive grove. The sloping ground ensures that surplus water flows away from these plants, which are planted randomly and bloom lavishly. If you visit a garden centre you will soon see that there are not only *germanica* hybrids.

This species and its varieties remain short. 'Aurea' is 15cm (6in) tall and yellow, 'Brassie' is golden yellow, 'Cyanea' dark blue, and 'Die Braut' white with creamy-yellow. All grow to about 10-25cm (4-10in) tall. These irises are good in pots, for example in a group on a wooden or stone table as a permanent item with some short annuals in separate pots. Do not put a saucer under them - let them drain well, particularly in the winter. They are also suitable in the foreground of not over-large borders. They really come into their own in slightly raised borders, which makes it is easier to observe their beauty.

Raising a border is, admittedly, a problem. For too long we have all been adept with railway sleepers and have lazily accepted these as the only solution. Now we are looking for alternatives that do exist. You can pile up lumps of peat to make an edge, though this is quite expensive. A hardened pine board can be nailed to small poles which are put into the ground to make a raised edge, small pieces of brick can be piled up, little walls can be made of clinkers, flagstones can be laid on top of one another in layers to form a wall, or you can use blocks of

Miscanthus *is an extended ornamental grass family, not all varieties of which flower in the climate of northern Europe, though* Miscanthus sinensis *'Silberfeder' does. You can fill whole gardens with the different varieties, as long as you have a good contrast in height between the groups.*

Left: Globe thistle, Echinops ritro *'Taplow Blue', is a sturdy grower which can reach the height of a human being.*

stone which have been specially cut for this purpose. These blocks of stone are ideal; they let the surplus water drain away between their cracks, are attractive in colour (reddish brown), and easy to stack. I recently made a large Japanese garden with them in Belgium. There was an old nut tree there which was too low for the future level of the garden, so I had a half-circle laid around it on two sides. This was a stacked wall made of blocks of natural stone. If you want to prevent the earth from escaping through the cracks, you must put a drainage sheet behind them – but it is better not to because irises love to nestle between the cracks of little walls where they find warmth and moisture in dry and cold periods.

I have already mentioned the irises at Italian farmhouses where they grow on walls. I think they must put earth on the walls and push the iris roots into it so that the tops remain in contact with the sun, otherwise the roots would rot away and they would not flower.

Iris in borders   Many plants grow upright with leaves that stand out horizontally, or there is a whirl of leaves as with *Geranium. Iris* makes a good transition between these two, the vertical and the round. The *I. germanica* hybrids, with leaves that are about 30-40cm (12-16in) tall and usually grey, are suitable as a striking vertical group, for example in the foreground of a very tall border and repeated in asymmetrical or symmetrical rhythmical groups.

A border with Iris germanica *hybrids in many tints during flowering (and also afterwards) offers a welcome break from the grass, which demands strong shapes.*

I. pumila hybrids can be put in slightly shorter borders, also at the front, or in very short borders with just creeping plants; then they can act as the connecting item between fanciful groups – even after flowering, when the foliage remains as a distinct emphasis. You will discover, after some study, that you can make magnificent colour combinations with iris flowers – there are plenty of *ugly* combinations to be seen in many gardens! If you want to play safe, choose blue garden irises and violet flowers for the violet corner, 'White Knight' for example for the white garden, and for the yellow garden the yellow *germanica* hybrids, such as the lemon-yellow 'Helge'. There is plenty of choice and, if you look into it, you will be confronted by a selection which is almost too great. I learned in the garden of Castle Walenburg that you can be disappointed, even if you have done everything possible to get irises to bloom. There in the herb-cum-cutting-flower garden, a pair of main paths which crossed one other were planted with *Iris germanica* hybrids. These cannot be brought into flower, in spite of all the advice of iris experts, and even though we dug them up, mixed the soil with sand to achieve better porosity, added lime, and re-planted the irises above the soil. Possibly the ground is not porous enough because the subsoil consists of heavy clay. If your garden consists of clay or other heavy soil, you can improve the water porosity by putting some rubble in the subsoil and trying to arrange the plant beds on a slightly higher level. Lay the plant beds on the slant and the paths

Liquid shades of columbines and Viola *'Vita'*.

Scabiosa caucasica *is lilac blue, while* S. c. *'Clive Greaves' is light blue and has large flowers.*

94

slightly lower, so that the rainwater will drain away from the surface via the paths. You might then be able to enjoy irises year in, year out. It is worth trying. Begin with a few plants or a group and, if it goes well, start collecting.

Iris kaempferi   A pond is often the focal point of a double border. It is fascinating to to see the reflections of the leaves of *Iris kaempferi* (which are also sword-shaped) in a pond. This iris is also known as Japanese iris, and I did in fact see many of them in Japan. There are two emperor's palaces in Tokyo. The present-day emperor lives in the older one. The other palace was built in western style and was inhabited by Emperor Meyji, who also had a European-style park laid out beside it. In this park there is a magnificent long *Iris kaempferi* garden situated beside a stream. Along one side of the stream is a broad path, which is definitely necessary in view of the thousands of visitors the garden attracts during the spectacular flowering period. The whole stream, which is 6-10m (20-33ft) wide in places, is planted with *Iris kaempferi*. The sea of deep purple, blue, and white forms an enormous expanse of flowers which are separated from one other in groups. It is my dream to recreate this one day in a garden. Visitors are led along both sides of the stream via bridges which join the two diagonally, so you can look at the stream from different angles. This makes visitors curious, and they keep following the stream because new compositions appear. The early-

Multi-coloured borders can also be subtle if the colours are separated by sufficient greenery. The Viola cornuta *hybrid 'Boughton Blue' stands in the foreground, combined with light blue* Delphinium.

95

flowering *japonica* azaleas stand on banks of earth which have been built up on each side. In this way the atmosphere of a mountain stream is created and attention is not diverted to other parts of the garden. The round shapes of the azaleas contrast splendidly with the sword-shaped leaves of the irises.

A Japanese iris garden in Belgium

I designed a large pond for a newly built extension to an existing house in St-Truiden in Limburg, Belgium. Broad-edged banks were incorporated into the design to create two possibilities. First of all I wanted to make it possible to plant wide borders of irises and, secondly, I wanted to let the gravel run gleaming into the water without sinking to the bottom of the pond. For this was to be a Japanese garden, or at least my interpretation of one. The thing which always fascinates me in Japanese gardens is the way the transition between water and land is effected.

Gravel continues up to the water's edge. Sometimes round pebbles are placed on a diagonal bank, or blocks of rock are positioned in such a way that they point out the transition from water to land. In other places the gravel bank continues under water. I wanted to introduce this effect in the Japanese garden in St-Truiden. Therefore gravel was alternated with broad strips of bank which were planted with Japanese irises. These water borders bloom profusely and bring back to me the memory of the Japanese stream garden in Tokyo's Meyji park.

Petasites albus, white butterbur, has white flowers in February and March.

Pretty grey foliage can be decorative and can even be very striking if you make largish groups of it. Santolina stands in the foreground with its yellow buds, behind it is Anaphalis with grey foliage and white flowers, and a clump of Artemisia forms the conclusion to the line.

More facts about irises

Iris pallida, Florentine iris, has sea-green/grey foliage and a lavender-blue flower. It looks wonderful in pale terracota pots on a large terrace. *I. p.* 'Variegata' is a must for lovers of variegated leaves. These leaves have a white border, while the flowers are light mauve. *I. sibirica* does not have large leaves but forms a thick bush. It is interesting to combine *I. sibirica,* which grows to a height of 70-80 cm (28-32in), with the *I. germanica* and *I. pumila* hybrids.

Plants with striking foliage
Inula, fleawort

The large oval leaves of fleawort hang slightly from the upright stems, which grow to a height of 1.5m (5ft) – at least in the fleawort which is seen most often, *Inula helenium,* the flowers of which are yellow and daisy-like. There is a wide-growing greeny-yellow species, *I.hookeri.* There are also short fleaworts, such as *I. ensifolia,* which is bright yellow, and *I. orientalis,* which is pure orange-yellow.

Hosta

Whole books have been devoted to the genus *Hosta,* of which there are many different species and varieties. The best known at the moment is *H. sieboldiana* 'Elegans'. The leaves of this variety are, together with those of *H. s.* 'Frances Williams', the largest that I know of in this family. The flowers are lilac and white and the leaves, which grow to around 50cm (20in) tall, are quite overpowering, not least because of their colour. *H. s.* 'Frances Williams' has the same blue leaves, but with a pale yellow border. This rather bizarre combination works only if it is

Rodgersia tabularis is called Astilboides tabularis *these days. The round leaves look like lotus leaves and stand on long stems.*

Following pages: Anyone who wants to keep a border tidy can surround it with a hedge of, for example, box, which does not always have to be as formal as in this garden. Not always logical at first sight but nevertheless often very attractive, is a combination of informal borders and plants surrounded by low box hedges.

Gunnera comes from Brazil, from the Amazon delta. Cover it with beech leaves and it will survive well so that you can enjoy its large leaves.

surrounded by a large number of blue and lemon-yellow flowers and very tranquil leaf shapes.

H. s. 'Frances Williams' can also be a striking single plant. One of the possibilities gardeners have is to arrange the garden entirely according to their own tastes and ideas. This is what Marcel Wolterinck did in Laren, North Holland – his inspiration for a garden surrounded by walls clearly came from Arabia and Tuscany. In his back garden (which is surrounded by tall trees), he built a high wall enclosing a rectangular space. This long section was divided in two by building a wall across it. The first garden was arranged as a terrace with a large table with a lead covering. Pots with yew globes were placed along the three walls. The space beyond this was covered with dolomite, or boulder clay, which created an ochre-coloured area. The walls were painted in the same ochre colour, which evoked the warm Tuscan atmosphere. Overhead, plane trees that have a horizontally trained system of branches on a stem of about 3m (10ft), branched out to form a green roof in the second space where they give welcome shade. Pots with *H. s.* 'Frances Williams' were placed along the walls. Only this sort of leaf was allowed which gives a welcome break from all the ochre colours.

H. tardiana has, if possible, even bluer leaves than *H. sieboldiana* 'Elegans'. You need to bring in a strong colour with it. The variety 'Halcyon' has smaller leaves than *H. s.* 'Elegans'. I once combined these two in a historic town garden.

Angelica is a good substitute for hogweed. It does not grow rampant and has splendid yellow curtains of flowers. Leave the seeds where they are and they will seed themselves.

Just imagine the following: a long, wide town garden behind a huge canal reach, with a splendid garden house at the end of the garden. Between the reach and the garden house is a formal garden which consists of four parts. One part is a large terrace with a broad box border across the whole width of the terrace. Gravel paths lead along it on the left and the right. Then there are paths which lead from left to right in between the plant beds. These plant beds are divided up by box hedges so that they have a border, a middle bed, and two side beds. In the middle bed I planted *H. s.* 'Elegans'; in the border which ran all the way round I put *H. tardiana* 'Halcyon'; and in the two side beds the pink rose 'Dainty Bess' was planted. So two blue-leafed hostas have been brought together to form a fascinating contrast. The smaller, bright blue leaves of the 'Halcyon' are placed opposite the larger leaves of the less blue 'Elegans'. Plant these hosta varieties in half-shade and not in very bright sunlight. This is a lesson I learned after a number of dry, witheringly hot summers, when the blue tints of the leaves became faded and greenish. You really need half-shade for blue. Besides H. tardiana 'Halcyon' there is the larger-leafed and taller-growing H. tokudama 'Hadspen Blue'. Two hosta varieties have firm, coloured borders to their broadly oval leaves: *H. fortunei* 'Aureomarginata', which has a golden-yellow border, and *H. crispula,* which has a white border. The tallest-flowering hosta is *H.* 'Krossa Regal', which blooms from early to late summer with splendid pale lilac bells which grow to a

Madeleine van Bennekom has a border in her garden in Domburg which attracts thousands of visitors every year, and which is an example to all plant-breeding gardeners. Blue-grey, and some yellow and pink, are combined here, and the deepest tints are the blues of Salvia, Viola, *and* Geranium.

99

good 1.2m (4ft). The leaves are also regal and large. Fortunately there are white-flowering hostas too, *H. plantaginea grandiflora*, which grows to a height of 50cm (20in), and *H. albomarginata* 'Snowflakes', which blooms 40cm (16in) tall. *H. a.* 'Alba' has small, lancet-shaped leaves and a flowering height of 60cm (24in). There is therefore plenty of choice for the white garden.

I have already mentioned two ways of using hosta: in pots as the main emphasis, or in a formal box garden as colour emphases or borders. In two perennial borders at Castle Walenburg, hosta provides a strongly rhythmical element at the front of the borders. To allow the leaves to develop, a border of paving stones or clinkers runs alongside the border as a boundary between grass and borders. The leaves thus remain undisturbed when the grass edges are clipped, and they can hang over the edge in a large tuft. We have planted the impressive *Hosta crispula* and *H. sieboldiana* 'Elegans' there. Around these are delicate-flowering plants, such as *Gillenia trifoliata, Gaura lindheimeri*, which are both white, and *Geranium psilostemon*, which is deep violet with a black heart. Knautia is also included with its purple *Scabiosa*-like flowers and the light blue *Geranium pratense* 'Mrs Kendall Clark'. Behind them come more plants with white flowers or light blue colours, such as *Campanula lactiflora* 'Loddon Anna', the *Phlox paniculata* hybrid 'Lavandelwolke', and the light blue *Delphinium* 'Berghimmel'.

Campanula *with an* Athyrium filix-femina, *lady fern, which stands out above* C. portenschlagiana *with its purple-blue flowers.*

Campanula latifolia macrantha *is purple-blue,* C. lactiflora *'Loddon Anna' is light blue. Cut away the clusters as they finish flowering. Then you will have the bonus of a second flowering.*

Many gardens in the village of Eext, in Drente, have been linked together into a coherent garden complex, which attracts more and more visitors each year. This garden has been created in various stages. For instance, an orchard was planted surrounded by three hedges, and after that a large terrace and four ponds with plant beds. Then a tranquil garden with hedges around it was added, in which hosta borders have been included in blue- and narrow-leafed varieties, and hortensias as background planting for late summer and autumn flowering. Two double iron arches with roses and ivy have been placed by the entrance and exit to this elongated garden. The central area is a long bed with ivy, out of which onions emerge with their twisted stems.

Helleborus This winter- and spring-flowering plant makes a true triumphal appearance in our gardens, and rightly so. There are two distinguishing marks which make its leaves so striking. The first is that there are species of Christmas roses which have very large leaves. *Helleborus lividus corsicus* (syn. *H. argutifolius*), for example, has very large, deeply incised leaves. These are green with a greyish-green film and a sharply serrated edge. The foliage looks bright amongst fresh green foliage and can be excellent in a shady border. The Christmas rose can also withstand sun, so it can be used anywhere. If you want seedlings from it, put them in a rather damp, shady spot. You can make large groups of them when the young plants have grown. Apart from

This shows how you can weave a touch of blue through a border of warm colours so that the blue will give a little tranquillity. In the front is cat mint, Nepeta, which has little grey leaves. The orange is provided by Kniphofia, red hot poker, while the white plume is an Artemisia lactiflora.

101

Delphiniums unfortunately bloom for only a short time - one month - but if they are cut back to ground level right after their first main flowering, they will bloom for a second time with almost the same abundance.

H. l. corsicus, which originates from the island of Corsica, there are other large-leafed varieties, such as *H. foetidus*, a wild Christmas rose from central Europe. I saw many of them in the Ardennes, mostly in airy oak woods. The shade under beech trees is too deep, and so Christmas roses will not grow there. *H. foetidus* has sharply incised leaves, divided like a hand, where each section of the leaf is longer than the next. After flowering, which lasts from December to April, the seedboxes appear, which are ugly once they have dried out and gone brown. Put plants around them which grow slightly taller so that the seedboxes are covered up and are out of sight when the rest of the border comes into flower. Then seedlings can be produced, at least if you put in some peat dust. The young shoots appear immediately after flowering and the old ones dry out into brown stems.

I have *H. foetidus* planted rhythmically in the middle of beds I look at all winter. This rhythmical arrangement seems unnatural, but I find it satisfactory as an eye-catcher. Usually you see wildish Christmas roses planted in separate groups under bushes, but I put them in borders for their foliage and winter-to-spring flowering. The greenish soft yellow flowers are a feast for the eye. There are two varieties of foetidus: *H. f.* 'Old', which grows to a height of 35cm (14in), and *H. f.* 'Wester Flisk', which grows to 50cm (20in). These are the best species with evergreen leaves. There are numerous other species and varieties which

Delicate plant forms: the Viola cornuta *hybrid 'Boughton Blue' blooms greyish blue.*

102

lose their leaves in the winter when the frost comes. Others keep their leaves for a long time in mild winters, but they do go an ugly brown with sharper frosts.

This is why all the leaves are often cut away in the winter so that the flowers can be enjoyed to the full at a time when white, pink, and violet-purple flowers are appreciated most, for example before those of *H. orientalis. H. purpurascens* flowers deep purple and has fresh green leaves.

Helianthus The perennial plant species *Helianthus,* well known as sunflower, blooms abundantly in yellow with daisy-like flowers and quite robust elongated leaves. The plants bloom at a height of 2m (6ft), are strong, and can withstand sun and dry conditions. They would soon take up the whole garden with their offshoots, which sprout from rhizomes. Simply pull up the surplus in the spring.

Besides this robust yellow-flowering foliage plant there are other tints, for instance *H.* 'Lemon Queen' and *H. decapetalus* 'Capenoch Star', which both flower lemon-yellow. *H. angustifolius* is light yellow and grows to a height of 2m (6ft).

Heliopsis *Heliopsis* has coarse, rather bumpy-looking, dull green leaf shapes and colours, with full golden-yellow flowers above them. Most varieties are 1.25m (4ft 2in) tall and do not differ from one another very much in

Keeping a border in colour for months on end is difficult. So choose long-flowering plants, such as Lavandula, Clematis, Ceonothus, Buddleia, *and* Salvia, *and for later in the year, autumn asters and* Ceonothus, *which retains its blue flowers for a long time.*

colour. They are strong plants, which produce perfect cutting-flowers that will last at least a week.

Gunnera   The largest foliage plant from our present-day garden stock is *Gunnera*. The leaves of *Gunnera* are palmate, deeply incised and rough, and grow to 3m (10ft) tall. This plant prefers to spread out widely along a water's edge, where it will produce an elongated, green fruit-cum-flower. Gunnera needs to be covered up in the winter. Put a wall of wire-netting around it and fill it with beech leaves. This is sufficient to prevent it from becoming damaged by the frost.

In the botanical garden in Edinburgh, I saw gunnera used in wide borders in a landscape form. There were large ponds and along the edges of them were these gigantic leaves, which were the eye-catchers in each group of plants. This suggests that you must also be fairly careful with them, since the leaves are so enormous that they can ruin all the other leaf forms.

Two plants which can stand up to the gigantic leaf shapes of gunnera are *Miscanthus sinensis* 'Giganteus' and *Darmera peltata*, with its large round leaves. Of course, butterbur can also be added to these, but there was none of this by the water's edge in the botanical garden in Edinburgh, while the other two were both there. By combining the large leaf and growing shapes with one another, something special was created. *Astilbe*, *Rudbeckia*, and *Kirengeshoma*, used in two large

A yellow and white border with pruned shrubs in the background, such as gold-variegated Ligustrum.

groups, formed a good contrast. On their own they would have been completely ineffective next to gunnera.

By building a white-painted brick wall around a small garden beside a white villa, a splendid patio was created with a Mediterranean air. In countries such as Spain, Italy, and Portugal you often see inner courtyards surrounded by white walls, which are then covered with all sorts of pots of geraniums, little orange trees, small palm species, and, of course, roses and bougainvillea.

It is curious that we associate geraniums with Mediterranean countries while, in fact, they are wild plants from South Africa. In the seventeenth century the geranium was brought from that country, where the *Pelargonium* still occurs naturally in many unknown varieties. In that little garden with the white wall around it there was a large gunnera, as the only plant of any size, with a collection of white daisies in pots on the terrace next to it. A white parasol completed the decorative, southern atmosphere.

The garden in Eext was different. A focal point was needed and a pond served this purpose. I am fascinated with the idea that the most beautiful section of the garden should be placed furthest away so it cannot be seen from the house: you have to walk through the entire garden to enjoy this beauty. The pond takes up the full width of the last section of garden, so that grass paths and narrow borders could be laid

There are several multi-coloured borders in Kensington Park, which have been filled with annual tuberous and bulbous plants. Dahlia *and* Salvia *are here in red splendour.*

at the extremities. A border was also put in beside the pond. This was quite wide, so there was room for two groups of lady's mantle, *Alchemilla mollis*, and *Darmera peltata*, and there was still space next to them for four large groups of gunnera.

These have grown tall in the mean time and, with the long pond, form the focal point. In the three corners of the pond, reeds of *Miscanthus sinensis* 'Gracillimus' elegantly bent outwards, as stately tall shapes were needed to restore the balance with the bushy leaf forms of the gunnera.

Left:
Genista aetnensis
grows extremely tall.

Filipendula

Filipendula is also known as spirea, and if you see the flower of this herbaceous plant (which is often planted to give height), you will see why. The stems are thin and elegant, the dull-green foliage is lobeate and rather elongated in shape. The leaves of the taller species are spaced far apart along the stems, and the shorter varieties have a stockier shape. On these stems appear the purple, white, or pink flower plumes which have given the plant the name of spirea. On marsh spirea, which has cream flowers, the flowers look like two drops of water. So if you want to make a transition from damp to dry, you can achieve this with marsh spirea in a damp spot and *Filipendula* in a dry spot. The tallest are *F. rubra* 'Venusta Magnifica' and *F. r.* 'Venusta'. The first has carmine red flowers, the second dark pink, and both grow to a height of 1.6m (5ft 6in). The species itself, *F. r.*, can even grow to

The yellow
Chamaecyparis *is*
neutralized here by
grey-leafed bushes
and perennials such
as Stachys byzantina.
Pink roses are
combined with them
and the red-leafed
smoke tree, Cotinus
coggyria *'Rubrifolius'*

2m (6ft). So plant them at the back of borders or as tall single plants with, for example, *Clematis recta,* the bush-like clematis which has innumerable little white flowers. The tall types also look good with the rather stiff phlox, bushes of autumn anemones, and other rather full, solid plant groups. There are also shorter species. *Filipendula purpurea* grows no taller than 60cm (24in) and has purple-red flowers, while *F. p.* 'Elegans' has carmine-coloured flowers. The latter two bloom for quite a short time and in a bushy form, quite differently from the rubra varieties, which are tall and elegant. The marsh spirea is called *Filipendula ulmaria,* and *F. ulmaria* 'Plena' has a full flower. Both have striking leaves.

The bluish foliage of Macleaya, *the tall plant in the background, combines well with blue-leafed* Hosta. *You can put any colour amongst these, although violet would perhaps be too bright with them.*

Eryngium *Eryngium,* or thistle, has found a permanent place in the garden with its striking foliage. *E. giganteum* is cultivated specially for its pure white foliage, which is so striking that they are nearly always left as single plants with wide-spread branches. They are best combined with blue or white flowers, and more grey-leafed plants, for example *Echinops,* the globe thistle, herbs such as *Artemisia,* and the silver-coloured leaves of *Salvia argentea.*

There are many further species with large, deeply incised green leaves, of which *Eryngium planum* 'Blauer Zwerg' is a frequently used variety which grows to a height of 60cm (24in) and has little bright blue flowers. It is attractive for refined bouquets and in the garden as a

separate group or as the transition between two quite heavy shapes, for example, of *Echinops*, the globe thistle, and white autumn anemones. A violet-blue *Eryngium, Eryngium zabelii* 'Violetta', grows to a height of 80cm (32in), its thistle-like flowers appearing on a ruff of splendid screening leaves. Flowering lasts for around two months, which is true for all *Eryngium*.

This is no ordinary plant, and its use requires some imagination. It has a wild character, which is why they are best woven amongst other groups of perennials as a wild separate group. Put *E. giganteum* slightly back from the edge of the border and then again slightly further in, in groups of three or five plants depending on the size of the border. You could possibly repeat this on the other side in a double border.

E. planum grows to a height of 1m (3ft) and therefore must be placed near the back, while *E. p.* 'Blauer Zwerg' goes perfectly amongst stiff *phlox, Chelone*, and bushes of *Geranium*, which are often too solid before and after flowering. The slender bluish branches add a certain amount of elegance.

Eryngium is indispensable in a blue garden, at least if it is sufficiently sunny and dry. It is ideal for difficult dry spots in the garden, and it makes a magnificent grey planting for your border with *Lavandula, Stachys*, and the short *Artemisia schmidtiana*.

*Leaf shapes are not
only decorative in
themselves, but
become even more
exciting when they are
combined with plants
that have much
smaller or differently
shaped leaves.*

Echinops

Echinops is a sturdy plant which grows to a height of 1m (3ft) in good soil and in a place that is not too dry or shady. Sometimes they dry out in the shade or become limp, which is not the intention; they are supposed to grow into an upright, full bush with incised feather-veined (elongated) leaves, which by itself is very striking. The globular, light mauve, blue-grey flowers are very enticing and are the refined pinnacle of this majestic plant. They are mostly seen in larger borders, owing to their volume and to the fact that the bottom of the leaf and flower stems is usually not so splendid. So plant other, shorter plants in front of them, such as *Polygonum amplexicaule*, *Gaura lindheimeri*, or *Lavandula* which go well with them as regards colour. The silver-leafed *Salvia officinalis* and the cultivated form *Salvia nemorosa* 'Ostfriesland' also look good with them. In old-fashioned borders the globe thistle is combined with tall *Achillea filipendulina* 'Coronation Gold'. With this combination you can take the orange route with *Alstroemeria* 'Orange King', or the blue with *Salvia.* There is also a shorter *Echinops,* which does not collapse so quickly and therefore does not have to be tied up. This is *E. ritro* 'Veitch's Blue', which is true blue and only grows to 80cm (32in).

Crambe cordifolia

Crambe cordifolia is one of the giants of the perennial world. The leaves are large, round, dark green, and somewhat elongated, and the flower stem is very tall with a sea of little white flowers above it. Besides

The giant butterbur is very much at home beside water and shows off the beauty of its leaves to the best advantage there. The plant flowers in early spring.

109

the green-leafed *C. cordifolia* there is the true sea kale which grows beside dunes and has blue-grey foliage that has a thistle-like appearance because of the curly leaves. Gardeners used to put terracotta pots to blanch them. Plant sea kale, *C. maritima*, in the border too, as a grey-blue group or in a row in the kitchen garden.

Cirsium This thistle-like plant is planted principally for the beautiful purplish colour of its flowers. The flower stems are green and long, so the thistle-shaped flowers stand distinct above the many elongated leaves. They are most effective planted as tufts amongst finer greenery or with grey leaves. A large group quickly becomes boring and untidy after flowering. *Cirsium japonium* 'Rose Beauty' is deep carmine and has flowers which are up to 80cm (32in) in height. *C. rivulare* 'Atro-purpureum' has purple, slightly violet-coloured flowers in a thistle shape.

It looks splendid with the ornamental grass, *Helictotrichon semper-virens*, which has grey leaves and grows into a very narrow, bushy plant with thin, arched reeds that rock in the wind because of their seedboxes.

Cimicifuga Bugbane is one of my favourite garden plants. I always get the most splendid flowers with *Cimicifuga racemosa*, which has quite robust, white spikes. The plants are long, stand straight upright, and have fine,

A farmhouse garden filled with tall yellow Achillea *and* Helenium *'Moerheim Beauty'. The little hedges consist of borders of* Saxifraga *and thrift,* Armeria maritima– *wonderfully old-fashioned.*

fernlike leaves. *C. dahurica* always blooms slightly less and later. The colour of the flowers is creamy white. This species grows to 1.5m (5ft) tall, while *C. racemosa* grows to 1.3m (4ft 3in). *C. simplex* is white and 1.3m (4ft 3in) tall, the same height as the abundantly flowering *C. s.* 'White Pearl'. For lovers of purple there is *C. racemosa* 'Atropurpurea', which has a secretive air because of its dark stems, its dark, finely incised leaves, and its white flower spikes. It looks magnificent with *Heuchera micrantha* 'Palace Purple', which has the same, or possibly a slightly redder leaf colour and white flowers that appear in fine, cloud-like clusters.

Brunnera *Brunnera* is an indispensable plant for a spring blue emphasis in the garden. The flowers are forget-me-not blue and bright. The leaves are large and round. The pure green leaf shapes become rather boring if they are in full sunlight and the foliage becomes dull. So give them a spot in the half-shade, where the leaves will remain fresh green. There are two varieties which have divergent leaf colours. *B. macrophylla* 'Langtrees' has foliage with light flecks and *B. m.* 'Variegata' has a broad white border around a green heart.

If there is any shade anywhere from a large rose bush, a silver-leafed *Elaeagnus angustifolia*, an elegant *Kolkwitzia*, a holly, or yew pillar, put *brunnera* underneath it so that they benefit from the shade. Try also to position them so that light shines behind the leaves, as they will

A white border beside a white dovecote, with Centranthus, Chelone, Polygonum, *and the grey-leafed* Anaphalis.

Left: Here is an inspiring combination in blue: Hydrangea micrantha *'Mariesii Perfecta' remains slightly purplish blue, while* H. serrata *'Bluebird' is a more pronounced blue.*

111

then show up brightly. Avoid large groups which need to grow in dry conditions and in bright sunlight, as the leaves are rather boring if you have to look at them all summer long. Even the blue flowers do not compensate for this. There are, of course, many answers to this. Plant slender-growing and summer-flowering plants with them, such as *Knautia* and *Gaura*, which both go on blooming for a long time, or put them next to spectacular plants such as *Cephalaria*, which has lemon-yellow scabiosa-like flowers on 2-2.5m (6-8ft) tall stems. Put brunnera underneath as a tranquil green foliage group; you can also do this with roses, with grey foliage plants, and with slender *Verbena patagonica*. If you want tranquillity in the summer, this is the perfect plant, which spreads easily and well.

The grey in this wide border links all the plants and stays looking beautiful for a long time, even when the flowers have almost finished blooming or are still to come into bloom.

Bergenia   For many people *Bergenia* provides an indispensable evergreen group in the border. The foliage goes a purplish colour, which is perfect for bunches of flowers in floating bowls. The flowers have been bright pink-violet from time immemorial and can be rather glaring, but in a garden in spring which is otherwise bare it gives a crisp spring greeting. There are also delicate colours, such as those of *B. ciliata* 'Illusion' (soft pink) and *B.* 'Silberlicht', which has white flowers with a pink glow. This plant is therefore not really suitable for a pure white and cream garden, but it is certainly a good spring-flowering plant. The leaves are always large, healthy, and leathery.

Our parents planted bergenias at the beginning of a border and we are still doing this. You will then do not have a bare winter start to the perennial garden. Put in one or more globes of box with them, and you will create a classic group. The winter scene can be extended with the grey of *Dianthus*, which lasts through the winter. Bergenias are also attractive on terraces because they produce long stems which creep across the ground and to some extent mask the sharp form of a terrace. They also do well in pots and containers, and in rock gardens, again in the foreground as a plant which softens the stark lines. Plant them in the sun or half-shade. My experience is that too much dryness leads to scrubby plants which keep getting smaller, instead of large fresh leaves and abundant flowering. Spray them, do not put peat dust in the plant hole, and spoil them a bit; you will get an excess of flowers and leaves in return for your trouble. The leaves take on extra colour if they grow in the sun; in the shade they remain fresh green. The purple leaves are magnificent with deep dark red or faded purple roses. If you like decadent arrangements, you will find a source of inspiration here.

Astilboides   The large round leaves really come into their own only in the shade or half-shade. If you have ever seen lotus blooming, you will know how the round leaves grow on a thin stem and rise up out of the water. *Astilboides tabularis* grows like this too, with round leaves, a thin stem, and a plume-like white flower, which can grow to a height of

1.2m (4ft). If you are making a shady border, or if part of your perennial border is in the shade, then it is a wonderful plant, which, together with ferns, *Cimicifuga*, and *Brunnera* can fill a whole corner in a decorative manner.

Artemisia I first discovered Artemisia as an ornamental plant in Margery Fish's garden at East Lambrook Manor. The garden was wild, with enormous 2m (6ft) tall *Cardiocrinum*, and a great deal of *Brunnera*, *Geranium*, and *Helleborus* in great bushy sections, which were combined with a little stream and pollarded willows. Behind a pink perennial garden was a border with exclusively silver-grey plants, which was something completely new at that time. Margery Fish had a small nursery with a special section for grey-leafed *Artemisia*. She discovered one species herself, and she gave it the name of *A. absinthium* 'Lambrook Silver' – a splendid light grey species with incised leaves and a height of 80cm (32in). This is the average height for most varieties, which are sometimes narrow-leafed, such as *A. ludoviciana* 'Silver Queen' that has incised elegant leaves. *A. ludoviciana*, which has broader leaves than *A. l.* 'Silver Queen', quickly becomes rather coarse. *A. absinthium* is another interesting species, which grows to a height of 80cm (32in) and develops into a bush which spreads to at least 1m (3ft). The branches are straight and dotted with striking grey leaf shapes so that you get the impression of a large bush. It is best to cut the plants back in

Campanula lactiflora *is built up here in a splendid cadence with white daisies on the left and yellow* Anaphalis *'Schwefellicht' on the right, which has little yellow flower heads. You can choose* Viola, Campanula, *or* Geranium *as short flowers.*

The labiate blossoms of Salvia *are a dreamy blue.*

May and possibly to repeat this once more before flowering, around July; then they will stay bushy and grow no taller than 70cm (28in). *A. arborescens* 'Powis Castle' also grows to about 70cm (28in) and is the same width or slightly narrower. Here too we are dealing with a robust bush of grey leaves, which are just as finely incised. There are many more attractive species and varieties. They are wonderful plants for colour effects amongst various leaves and they hardly ever look wrong with the flowers of perennial plants, roses, or shrubs. And yet you should not over-use them as they break up the harmony of the green, which takes away the tranquillity if this happens too often. So be sparing with them and use them as a theme for part of the border. If you want to take things to extremes, you can arrange a whole grey garden, with lavender, *Stachys*, *Helianthemum nummularium* 'The Bride' (white), and *Eryngium giganteum* (blue thistle). I mix, for example, the medium height *A. absinthium* 'Powis Castle' and very short varieties such as *A. schmidtiana* and put amongst them pink-, blue-, and white-flowering plants, which should preferably be bushy. All stiffness is removed by the grey leaf colour, and a fairytale vision created.

Angelica   Angelica develops into a very tall plant (easily 2m [6ft]), and its flower stem is covered in a curtain of greeny-yellow flowers and later yellowish seeds. It is a good substitute for hogweed. *Heracleum* used to be very popular, but was renounced because of its untameability and

The upright flower shape of Verbascum chaixii *'Album' bears flowers for a long time.*

The foremost red border, in my opinion, is the one at Hidcote Manor. Here you can stand eye to eye with Canna, Dahlia, roses, annuals, and perennials, all red.

because the poison in its stems could cause burns. Angelica has been around for centuries. The leaves are sharply incised and broadly overhanging, so a great deal of space is needed for it. After flowering there are rather untidy seeds. Collect some of them and cut off the surplus, otherwise the whole garden will soon be full of *Angelica*. Sow the seed in situ or in pots so that a good clump comes up. A compact clump of plant can be replanted where it is required.

Angelica lends a distinct emphasis to the large herb garden of Pieter Baak and Frank Linschoten. It stands in a roomy corner, in front of a tall beech hedge. If the stems are bent by a gust of wind it does not really matter, because there are plenty of plants such as marsh-mallow, fleawort, chicory, and monkshood in the neighbourhood to divert the attention. The lay-out of the herb garden formed part of a total concept created for the large grounds of which this garden forms a part. Two rectangular beds, situated one behind the other, were put in for short herbs such as *Santolina,* sage, chives, and rue – all plants that are best kept short. They are pruned into little hedges here. In the middle of these two beds were placed junipers, one bush in each, which must have grown to 2m (6ft) by now. They are slim, greyish pillars which remain green in winter and are therefore important when the herbs collapse. Juniper berries are used in meat dishes, so they belong with the herbs. Along the sides of this elongated herb garden are the tall

In the middle is white Crambe cordifolia, and in front the grey of Artemisia ludoviciana, which has quite wide leaves.

herbs, which are divided from the central part by clinker paths. There is another axis, a grass path. The garden as a whole is quite complicated, but as you wander round here everything becomes obvious – that is proof that it works.

Angelica is, for a time, the tallest herb in the garden. The stems can be dipped in sugar water and used as a garnish for gateaux and desserts.

I have *Angelica* in my garden in Zeeland. From the shell terrace (which is surrounded on two sides by the old walls of my house and on the other two sides by broad, low box hedges), I look out on to my herb garden. It is a long garden with a view on to water and meadows, and therefore not an enclosed garden. To create extra depth, I planted angelica at the front of the strips of plants. The grey of the *Artemisia* fades away into the distance of meadows and trees, as does the blue-flowering hyssop. You can create depth by placing the large leaf forms at the front and the small and grey-leafed plants at the back.

Anemone Few plants are so often present in a perennial garden as autumn anemones. This is due to the colour of the flowers, which is always modest and delicate: white, pink, and dark pink. This bush-like plant grows from a well developed clump that is full and robust in shape, and has leaves that develop into three points, one long and two shorter. The advantage of this bushiness is that a wall of green is created, around which more delicate plants can be placed. *Anemone* is not happy in my

Telekia speciosa grows tall, and has golden-yellow daisy-like flowers and broad elongated leaves. On the right is the tall Macleaya.

garden on the clay, which is dry in summer. It almost dries out, which means that a spot in the half-shade is always to be recommended. Anemone blooms in the second half of the summer and produces flowers into the autumn, if the circumstances are right. Otherwise it stops flowering.

My favourite of this vast genus is *A. hybrida* 'Honorine Jobert'. It blooms white with a yellow heart and is an indispensable flower in a richly varied border or in a white, blue and white, or white, pink, and blue flower border. Its height is 90cm (36in). Flowering lasts a long time, and begins at the end of July. *A. hybrida* 'Lady Gilmore' is slightly shorter and has pink flowers. *A. h.* 'Queen Charlotte' is half-full, also pink, and the same height as *A. h.* 'Lady Gilmore', which blooms singly. *A. h.* 'Elegans' is single and pink and also 90cm (36in) tall. Darker tints can be found in *A. hupehensis,* such as *A. h.* 'Splendens', which is dark pink. *A. h.* 'September Charm' is also dark pink, while *A. h.* 'Prinz Heinrich' has deep purple-pink flowers. They are half-full, which detracts to some extent from the simplicity of the flowers, but it is very welcome for a rather decadent garden planting. In the Victorian era full flowers were popular, so they go well with garden styles which date from this period. They make magnificent colour combinations with light pink *Lavatera* 'Barnsley' and *Monarda* 'Prärienacht', and *A. h.* 'Prinz Heinrich', which grows to a height of 80cm (32in), goes

In Amsterdam I once designed a garden for two houses to create one large front garden. Lavender, Salvia nemorosa *'Ostfriesland,' and* Nepeta *are combined here as blue flowers with* Campanula lactiflora*. The rose is the iron-strong* 'Iceberg'.

White cluster and climbing roses are combined here with blue delphiniums, with tufts of grey from bushes such as Salix repens nitida *and* Pyrus salicifolia.

wonderfully well with them. A very strong species of the *Anemone* family is *A. tomentosa*, which has several varieties that nearly all grow to a height of 80-100cm (32in-3ft). *A. t.* 'Albadura' has white flowers with some pink on the outside, *A. t.* 'Robustissima' has bright pink flowers. *A. t.* 'Superba' is bright pink and flowers abundantly for a long time.

There really ought to be an autumn anemone in every border, and preferably several groups in different tints of pink and white. Put the taller species and varieties which I have described at the back, with slender leaves or flowers in front, and a few very large leaf shapes right at the front of the border, as the coarseness of the anemones needs to be broken up by distinct accents, or by having a large number of delicate plants with them, such as *Thalictrum* or *Clematis recta*, which has myriads of small white flowers. Large forceful plants can also be put with *Anemone*, for example *Rheum tanguticum*, *Crambe cordifolia*, and *Rodgersia* in half-shade.

Actaea pachypoda

We do not often see *Actaea pachypoda* in gardens; this must be because it is not well known. However, once you have seen the jade grey green berries, you will want this plant in your garden. It is not a particularly difficult plant, as long as you give it humus and shade, or even deep shade. This rather bushy plant with finely incised fresh green leaves that together, however, are robust and large, reaches a height of

Winter in the garden with snow-covered ornamental grasses. Even the evergreen bamboos hang their branches. They do not break, but simply bend because of the frost.

70cm (28in). The berries stand out just above the leaves on elegant stalks. Put them at the front, otherwise you will not see the berries. Use them therefore as single plants or in a large group with tall autumn anemones, *Macleaya*, or bamboo bushes behind them. A very refined effect can be achieved by putting short grey plants with them, which allows the jade colour to come out amongst the leaves.

Acanthus
Acanthus is a very decorative flowering and foliage plant which likes sun. This is not so strange when you consider its place of origin, Asia Minor. The Greeks first used the pattern of the foliage for embellishing their columns and this form has been copied endlessly. The plant itself began its triumphal march into our gardens slightly later. In many borders a large area has been cleared for the large, deeply incised leaves and the tall flower stems with their large labiate flowers. The upper labiates are purple and the under labiate white. Most often seen is *A. mollis*, which has rather coarse incised elongated leaves. *A. spinosus* has deeply incised leaves, which are extraordinarily beautiful.

In southern England, close to the famous gardens of Sissinghurst Castle and Great Dixter, is a medieval castle. There is a large hall with banners where the whole court used to eat, and there are magnificent rooms with four-poster beds and embroidered curtains and bedcovers. The garden is partly formal, with roses, box, and lavender, and partly

Multi-coloured large-scale borders are planted underneath old apple trees with all the colours next to one another in large groups (Penshurst Place, Kent).

modern, consisting of theme gardens designed by the famous post-war landscape gardener Sylvia Crowe. What I have always remembered and what has very much inspired me is the entrance to this famous garden. This consists of a long path along which carriages, and now and then cars, can drive. Broad strips of plants have been arranged as borders on each side, with a hedge as background.

The unusual thing is that, at regular intervals, there are old fruit trees with tall trunks. They must have already been there before the borders were designed. Because of their open structure the trees let enough light through for phlox, marguerite daisies, *Heliopsis, Geranium, Alchemilla, Echinops,* and large groups of *Acanthus mollis,* which mark the beginnings and ends of the borders. They stand in the half-shade of the trees with marguerites, looking bright because of their leaves and even more so because of their flowers, which appear next to one another as tall vertical shapes along upright stems.

When flowering is over, the black fruits appear, which are just as splendid. By choosing rather simple perennials, which have a rustic air but are nevertheless good in variation with one another, the entrance path is swathed in an atmosphere of simplicity, which at once sets the tone for the whole garden. Everything is pure and well chosen, partly owing to the *Acanthus* shapes.

Views through here have been made as radii, with a blue flower border in the middle, of which Nepeta *and* Lavandula *form the foreground.* Lavandula angustifolia *'Munstead' is light blue, and so is* Nepeta faassenii.

121

A garden in Schuddebeurs

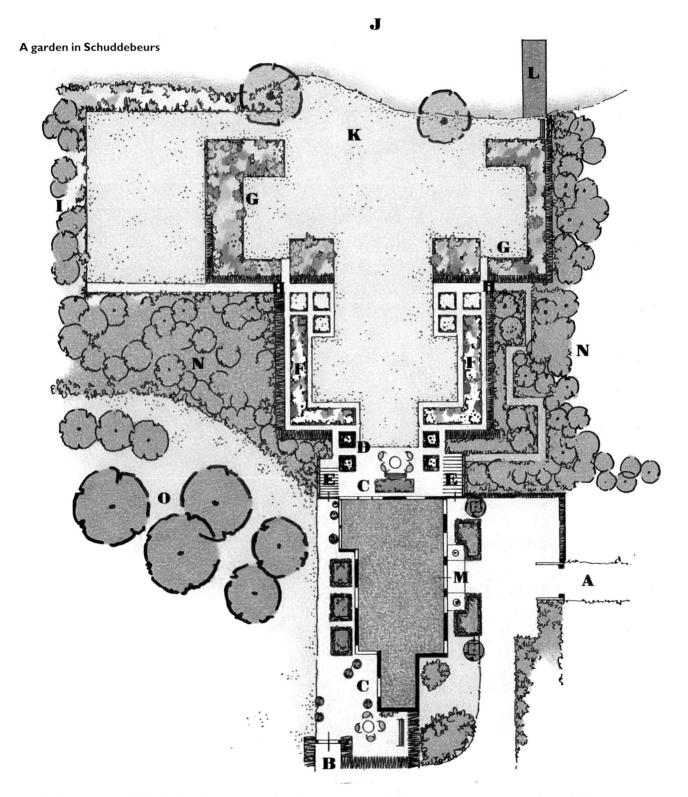

A the front entrance which leads through a
  little wood

B the back entrance which leads to the
  stables and barns

C terraces

D box hedges with white standard and
  bush roses

E hardwood pergolas, symmetrically
  positioned

F grey, blue, and white borders with a
  single pink tint

G pink borders

H yew hedges

I yellow garden

J the remains of an earlier burst dyke

K grass with willows

L a landing stage for fishing or dreaming

M the front door

N bush plants

O large lawn with old chestnut trees

Perennials in place of weeds

Various traditions have developed in landscape gardening that are connected with certain countries or certain parts of the world. For instance, England is the country of perennial borders because this is where the idea came from.

Some countries are noted for slender transparent forms, which are achieved by careful control of the height and shape of the plants. Countries such as China, and particularly Japan, are masters of this art and have shown us the way to prune, cut back, and cut asymmetrical bushes into shape. Irregularity of shape is of prime importance in these countries. Whereas in England it is important for combinations of perennials to resemble bunches of flowers – in other words, full, rich groups of plants close together without soil showing in between – in Japan a different principle is paramount. This is the idea of a mossy area with an irregularly pruned *Pinus* standing above it.

Whether small or large, the important thing is that the tree is pruned in layers so that you can see through it. The ground beneath must be flat and must in no way detract from the shape which hovers above it. Moss is possibly the shortest known plant for covering the ground and it is felty green.

Astilbe soon achieves medium height in a small garden. Plant wide groups of it, if you have the space, and they will cover the shady, preferably rather damp, ground like a blanket.

Moss as the shortest ground cover

One of the reasons I went to Japan was to discover the secret of transparency and space, which they seem able to achieve in both large and small gardens.

I went on a trip to some small tea gardens, which are sometimes part of a larger lay-out or sometimes belong to a convent or a restaurant. It is a distinct style: the tea-house, or rather, the tea-garden style. A permanent ingredient is a pavilion-like building in which you sit on low

Tall vertical groups such as Verbascum, Eremurus, *and* Digitalis *look best rising out of a patch of short* Geranium, Sedum, *and* Prunella. *The contrast is spectacular and surprising. Here you can see king's spear,* Eremurus.

cushions. The tea master or mistress prepares and pours the tea. Outside, the area is small and shallow, or slightly deeper. You can see this at its most beautiful in the garden of Murin An in Kyoto.

Just imagine: you sit in a pavilion with several rooms on each side that are closed off by sliding walls, and you look into a deep garden. What you see is moss and a little stream of water which flows towards the pavilion via many levels.

The garden, therefore, is high at the back and lower at the front. Round stones have been laid in the stream to create little waterfalls. The moss grows wonderfully here, and is a fresh downy green. There is not just one species but many, which all shine slightly differently. Moreover, the colour is brilliant in rainy weather. On the moss along the boundary are many trees, which are narrowed down to evergreen bushes at the furthest extremity of the garden. A few maples and fir-trees stand out of the woods as single trees in the garden.

A single fir-tree is pruned into a shape which brings a horizontal aspect to the design, for it is well known that maple, fir, and Japanese cherry all like to grow upwards (in other words, vertically) as quickly as possible. The maple bushes are trimmed to allow as much light as possible to penetrate underneath for the moss.

The general impression is natural and tranquil, and the lesson I learned is that you can make a fascinating garden lay-out with just one ground-cover plant, moss.

Rhythmical ground-cover plants are grouped to left and right of the flagstone path. Bergenia with its round green leaves is a valuable foliage plant at all times of the year. It flowers early and is pink-violet.

How do you get moss?

In Europe people often complain about moss in grass and between plants, but in Japan they would be pleased with so much moss. Moss is usually found growing on thickly covered ground, for example where many trees drop their leaves. Then the ground gets hardly any oxygen, which no longer gives weeds a chance. Personally I usually advise people to gather moss in the wild, to cut it finely or to pull it up, and then to push it firmly into closely rolled or trodden-down ground.

Use clean river sand and mix it with a bit of peat. The topsoil will then remain damp for a long time. Spray regularly, preferably with fine watering roses. You must bring tranquillity to the area. The ground with the moss on it must be strewn with some sand and peat dust, the same amount of each, and again rolled or trodden down lightly. This is most successfully done with a not too heavy grass-roller. Make sure there is some shade, because moss dries out quickly, particularly if it has not been in place very long. Moss has no roots, so it can also grow on a stone wall or paving stones. Put a few maples above it or a splendidly shaped *Prunus*, preferably a small-flowered one, and you will create a special corner in your garden as a welcome and restful change from the beds and borders with their varying degrees of colour.

If you convert a kitchen garden like this into an ornamental garden you must choose plants which spread as they grow and preferably choke all the weeds.

Lady's mantle seeds itself plentifully, so you can fill whole areas with it.

Important ground-cover plants

The wooden floors of pavilions such as one sees in Japan have had a certain influence on a whole new "un-English", but still very inspiring, form of landscape gardening. In this sort of design large square wooden

platforms, for example, are used for terraces, which lead into one another in the garden. Sometimes the idea is restricted to a simple red wooden terrace behind the house, which is bordered by grass, short plants, and single shrubs.

The basic principle of this modern landscape gardening is not to create as much variety as possible in perennials, inflorescences, or colour nuances of flowers. What counts is the feeling of space. This is especially important for smaller garden surfaces. If you do not want to become claustrophobic from over-full perennial borders, you need to create space.

Single plants, such as *Nothofagus, Rhus typhina*, (sumach), and *Salix matsudana* 'Tortuosa' (hoary willow) came into vogue, all of which are bushes that do not flower, are irregular in shape, and create tranquillity and space. The effect should be oriental without the work necessary for creating elegant, Japanese bush shapes. Some of these very sturdy ground-cover plants are also magnificent and easy to maintain. They look perfect in beds and borders, especially along the edges if they remain short, but their use goes further still. Large surfaces of ground-cover plants ensure that there is both tranquillity and variety in beds and borders.

A garden beside a watermill, which is situated high up in relation to the damp, low-lying land. A long border is the perfect cover here for the heavy loess, on which everything appears to thrive and which withstands damp in the winter.

The garden of Kiftsgate Court in the Cotswolds is open to the public.

Above: Hosta.

Left: A stately and rather static path with conifers can be livened up with Bergenias.

Acaena (New Zealand burr, pérri-pérri-bur)

Possibly the flattest ground-cover plant of the perennials. The inflorescence is on average about 10cm (4in) tall and consists of little reddish globes that are situated on short stalks, embellished with innumerable tiny hairs which stick out. The foliage is fine, fernlike, green and grey. The plant likes the sun and ground which is not of too poor a quality. *Acaena buchananii* has greyish-green foliage; *A. caesiiglauca* is blue-green, which looks splendid with *Crambe maritima*, sea kale, and *Helictotrichon sempervirens*, the blue grass with the elegant reeds. *A. microphylla* has bronze-coloured leaves which look beautiful with lady's mantle and with the brown leaves of *Ligularia*.

A. m. 'Kupferteppich' has slightly browner leaves; it would be a good idea to put the evergreen globe-grass *Festuca scoparia* amongst it in a group or as a single plant. *A. novae-zelandiae* has the largest leaves of all the *Acaena* and is 20cm (8in) in height including the flower.

Ajuga (bugle)

A splendid ground-cover plant. My experience is that they do not have the desired effect in dry spots; shade is less of a problem, even deep shade, but dry conditions are bad. The blue flower of *Ajuga*, which blooms at a height of 10cm (8in), is splendid; the plant is bare in winter and has bronze-coloured green leaves. *A. reptans* 'Alba' is white. *A. r.* 'Multicolor' has variegated leaves: the leaves have white flecks, which I often find rather sickly, but

they can be surprising if used well. The tallest *Ajuga* is *A.* 'Jungle Beauty', which grows to a height of 30cm (12in).

Alchemilla

A slightly taller ground-covering perennial. The flowers are like something from a fairytale, with many small yellow star-shaped florets which "float" above the ground like clouds. Before and after flowering there is the felty grey-green foliage, which always looks as if it has a raindrop inside it. Many gardening fanatics cut off the leaves and the flowers straight after the first flowering, and so get a second flowering. I have not been successful with this on my Zeeland clay and in the sun, but I keep trying on a small scale. If you have good rich earth which is damp and half in the shade, you will be sure to succeed. The secret seems to be to cut off all the leaves and flowers at the end of June, and the fresh green leaves will be there after your holiday. There is a short *Alchemilla* for large groups in the foreground of a border, *A. alpina*, which grows to a height of 25cm (10in), and an even shorter variety, *A. erythropoda* (20cm [8in]). The well-known *A. mollis* grows to a height of 40cm (16in). The leaves of the two former species are smaller, and so is the inflorescence, so they are suitable for small gardens. *Alchemilla* is the ideal ground cover, particularly for planting under bushes and single plants and under formal roses, but it has one disadvantage: it spreads. There is a lot to be said for cutting them back quickly when the flowers start to go brown. Personally, I cut them off

slightly before and dry them, so that I can make large bunches of them in the winter, with the soft yellow as the basic colour.

Alyssum

A good ground-cover plant which has bright yellow flowers in the early spring. The leaves remain greyish-green. Find it a dry sunny spot.
Arabis is the earliest spring-flowering perennial if you do not count those which flower in the winter.
It is a true rock garden plant, which likes dry conditions and sun.
I found plants of it here and there in my farmhouse garden, which have mauve-blue flowers. I put them on a patch of rubble in the ground which I could not reach with the shovel and they are doing wonderfully.
Sometimes I really think that they

scarcely make roots and have a "self-supporting" system of little roots, which just sit in the topsoil and do not need to go deep.
This is their secret: it appears that a little dust is enough for them to live on. With sun and good drainage they bloom abundantly from March until well into May.
The colours are blue-mauve-pinkish; they are short and the plant grows rampant in an attractive manner.

Armeria maritima (thrift)

A little wild plant from the salt marshes. There are many species which have white or pink flowers. They all form clumps of dark green grass, which slowly spread into a small patch of carpet. *A. m.* 'Alba' is white-flowering, *A. m.* 'Düsseldorfer Stolz' is carmine red, and *A. m.* 'Rosea' is pink.

Here four pointed yews have been put together at an intersection of paths. Beside them are delicate plants, such as violet Penstemon *and grey* Salvia. *There are also a bergamot plant and* Sidalcea *in the main colour, violet.*

Opposite page: Newby Hall near York has several sorts of gardens which certainly justify a visit. This is the rock garden with a little brick wall and a jumble of Salvia, Artemisia, Geranium, Dianthus, *and* Sedum, *which like this dry, porous spot.*

Artemisia schmidtiana

Remains 20cm (8in) tall, even when the plant spreads out. Find a sunny, dry, well drained position for this silver-grey, very fine-leafed plant, and a miracle will unfold before your eyes: the most delicate leaves will form a downy blanket between the rather coarser perennials. In my garden on heavy clay this *Artemisia* survives all the damp, cold, and wind, so perhaps its need for well drained ground is a myth.

Aster

Often called autumn aster, because the flowers do not come into flower until the second half of the summer or beginning of autumn.
There are tall and also plenty of short species and varieties in all colours of white, pink, blue, and mauve, but not yellow. The *Aster dumosus*

varieties, in particular, are short.
A. d. 'Snowsprite' is white,
A. d. 'Lady in Blue' is blue,
A. d. 'Alice Haslam' is pinky red, and
A. d. 'Lavanda' is lavender blue.

Astilbe

Also called *Filipendula* or spirea. Its plumed type of flower is slender and almost indefinable because of the many small florets. It is a haze of flowers. With my favourite, *A.* 'Sprite', which flowers rather more compactly in a stony-pink colour, the haze is replaced by an abundance of rather open, vertical flower shapes that remain more transparent because of this. There are white species and varieties, such as *A.* 'Deutschland', 50cm (20in) tall, and also all colours of pink, purple, red and white. Preferably, choose your variety when you see a plant in

flower as shades are often glaring and there can be a great difference and often too great a contrast between red, carmine, and purple, which creates a clashing effect.
A. chinensis 'Pumila' comes from China and is the shortest variety. It flowers to a height of 30cm (12in), including its leaves, and likes sun and half-shade. *A.* 'Inschriach Pink' has fresh-pink flowers and grows to 35 cm (14in). Do not put *Astilbe* in bright sunlight but in a rather cool, not over-dry spot in the shade or half-shade, and you will have intense enjoyment from it, not least because of the fernlike leaves that give great delicacy to this ground-cover plant after flowering.

Aubrieta

Grows very short, to about 20cm (8in). The plant is 10cm (4in) tall

A boundary wall of grey natural stone has created two levels.
Above: Chelone obliqua *is a perennial.*
Left: a globe of yew has been planted here as a break.
Opposite page: the white Verbascum chaixii *'Album'.*

without the flowers and is often grey leafed. It is ideal for a blue, pink, and violet garden, as there are many shades which flower very early from March to May. Give it a rather dry, sunny spot and you will enjoy this ground-cover plant that is regarded by many people as a rather old-fashioned country plant that blooms at a time when there is still hardly anything else in flower. A. 'Double Stock-flowered Pink' is pink, A. 'Drayton' purple, A. 'Lavender' lavender blue.

Bergenia

A good feature is its ground-covering character. Plant it in rich ground, preferably in the sun, and a certain amount of moisture will do no harm, even though you also find it among stones in rock gardens. The roots find the necessary moisture and

warmth between the stones. The colours are pink, white, and violet, and the leaves are evergreen.

Campanula

Several ground-cover species and varieties of this plant can look splendid at the front of a border. *C. carpatica* is about 25cm (10in) tall and is available in the colours white, light blue, and dark blue. *C. portenschlagiana* is blue-violet; it goes on flowering for a long time if the flowers which have finished are cut off; new flowers will appear and this keeps happening until well into the autumn. *C. poscharskyana* is the same height and flowers blue-violet. These are plants for sun and half-shade; they are also good beside the edge of a pond, which they will completely overgrow. There are many other varieties in all shades of

blue and white, but do not make the mistake of buying one of each sort, because the image you then create will not be restful.
Always choose large groups; this keeps the garden distinct and tranquil.

Cerastium

Grows low over the ground with fine stems and small grey leaves.
The little flowers are white. Sun is a requirement for this delicate rampant-growing plant, which can have very long stems and is thus suitable for large areas or for hanging over little walls.

Convallaria majalis

The indomitable lily-of-the-valley, a romantic name for a splendid foliage plant.
The stems appear early in the spring

with the delightful-smelling flowers; after that come the elongated leaves, two at a time on each stem. The plant has underground root shoots, so in good rich shady situations there are soon whole patches of them. If you want to have these, you must give them space, under deciduous shrubs, for example. Pick plenty of them and enjoy the scent, which is incomparably sweet. If you have a small garden without beds or paths you will eventually find the plant a nuisance because of its rampant character.

You can limit it with a path or other strong plants in a border which grow so thick and tall that they stifle the leaves.

For this you could consider *Mahonia, Stephanandra, Symphoricarpos,* and *Hedera helix* 'Hibernica' (bush ivy).

Corydalis squalida

Has fine, fernlike, small leaves which tumble over one another. You can actually walk on this plant, so it is suitable for spots where you need to prune a hedge or where you want to clip a Japanese *Pinus,* for instance. There are no flowers, so it is purely a matter of the fine green leaves. They look marvellous under a fanciful *Enkianthus campanulatus,* or an *Acer palmatum,* where they create tranquillity and space; why should you not fill half your garden with them? Flowers can sometimes give a restless impression, so if you like Japanese garden art this is a good substitute for mossy vegetation.

Dianthus deltoides

The rock carnation, a short, creeping plant with small violet star-shaped flowers. This plant looks good with

Eryngium giganteum, the blue sea thistle, or with *Verbena patagonica,* which rocks at a height of about 1.25m (4ft 2in) with purple flowers on a thin stem. There is also a white variety. I combine them in my garden with lavender, which is often rather coarse and compact whereas the short rock carnation is fine and delicate. There is also a white *D. d.* 'Albiflorus'. The brides' carnations, which are used for bridal bouquets, also come in many colours from white to violet and pink. They are evergreen or, rather, grey, which is greatly enriching. All carnations like sun.

Dicentra (bleeding hearts)

This plant is good for half-shade where the leaves stay a beautiful fresh green. Select the *D. eximia* varieties as ground-cover plants and for a position at the front of the border. *D. e.* 'Alba' is white, *D. eximia* with no variety name is pink. *D. formosa* 'Bountiful' is 25cm (10in) tall and has beautiful bluish leaves, while the other *Dicentras* have greenish leaves. This plant is of great value in creating the effect of space.

Dryas suendermannii

I once found this in the Swiss mountains. Alpine plants often grow tall on good ground, but this little evergreen plant remains short and has white flowers up to a height of about 10cm (4in) tall. The leaves are a rather greyish green.

Fragaria vesca

The wild strawberry. You seldom still see these little plants in the wild, but you sometimes find them beside streams or in damp woods. The leaves are fresh green, the flowers white, and the fruit small and sweet. They can produce magnificent rampant growth under bushes, which never grows tall and forms a field of fresh green leaves. These scented wild strawberries are very effective as decoration for gâteaux and fruit. They cannot withstand very dry conditions, but are fine in deep shade.

Geranium

Many species are tall or medium height, but there are also short ground-cover species. In a large garden they are almost all short because they grow broadly and are bushy. *Geranium pratense*, the wild violet-coloured *Geranium* with the fine leaves, blooms continuously and is often seen in southern Europe.

It combines well with roses, lavender, and with all sorts of rather bushy perennials, which check it in its forward march. Another short variety is *G. dalmaticum*, which has pink flowers, dark green foliage, and grows no taller than 15cm (6in). *G. cinerium* 'Ballerina' is 20cm (8in) tall and light carmine-violet. It blooms in the early summer. The *G. clarkei* varieties grow taller. *G. c.* 'Kashmir White', which has the most beautiful leaves and fine white bells, is 35cm (14in) tall. There are also purple and pink versions of *G. c.* 'Kashmir Purple', which stay at the same height and bloom only once. *G. endressii* remains 30-40cm (12-16in) tall and continues blooming with little light grey-violet-pink flowers, which show up in the dark. Cut them back partially or completely after the first flowering and new

If you want individual ground-cover plants you should try short roses, such as 'The Fairy', which blooms for a long time, and mix them with grey-leafed Salvia officinalis, *short* Artemisia, *and* Anaphalis.

Opposite page: Salvia officinalis *'Purpurascens' has purple and grey leaves and forms a distinct break from the rest of the short perennials which, even if they are not in bloom, are still fascinating because of their round shapes.*

leaves will appear – and often more flowers too. The violet-coloured *G. endressii* 'Wargrave Pink' grows pleasantly rampant in places where large groups are needed that will go on blooming without problems. This plant needs half-shade or deep shade. The leaves more or less disappear in the winter, but it shoots early. The flowers come in May to June. *G. macrorrhizum* flowers once abundantly and after that displays just its beautifully shaped leaves. There is a white variety, *G. m.* 'Album', and a pink one, *G. m.* 'Spessart'. *G. sanguineum* is less tall and comes in various colours; the species *G. sanguineum* itself is carmine red, *G. s. striatum* is pink, *G. s.* 'Jubilee Pink' magenta-pink, and *G. s.* 'Shepherd's Warning' white and pink. *G. sanguineum* has a rustic air and is ideal ground cover.

You could fill a book with these geranium species and varieties. They are just as popular with lovers of rock gardens as with border fanatics, so seek and you will find what you want in the way of colour, height, or leaf shape.

Helianthemum (rock rose)

This sun-lover is content with a place between flagstones, clinkers, or chunks of stone, where it is warm and moist. The site must be porous if you want to keep the plants through the winter. They often stand in too much water and rot in the winter and in the spring. There are many pink colours, such as *H.* 'Lawrenson's Pink'; *H.* 'The Bride' is white with grey leaves, *H.* 'Salmon Queen' is orange-apricot, *H.* 'Cerise Queen' is carmine-pink, and *H.* 'Yellow Double' (which has double flowers)

is yellow. They stay short; if they are in a place which is too wet or too shady they soon drop. However, if you have a sunny, porous spot in your garden you can get endless enjoyment from these slender foliage plants with their *Cistus*-like flowers, which keep on blooming. I suspect the *Helianthemum* of being a wild Mediterranean plant too, and have often seen them during journeys in Italy.

Helleborus

Makes a good background with its 30-50cm (12-20in) tall inflorescences and leaves, which are a tranquil green in the summer. In the winter and early in spring you have the flowers and the leaves, which cover the ground well. If you have the money and space, make large groups of them. Unfortunately the plants are

The garden of Chartwell, Kent, which Churchill walked through every day, is open to the public.
Left: Salvia, *sage, and* Sedum album *'Murale'.*
Opposite page: Short perennials grow in patches.

expensive, so it is a question of setting priorities or extending the groups gradually.

Hosta

They are all ideal ground-cover and border plants because their leaves shut off light from the earth so that no weeds can grow in between. Moreover, they keep growing into larger clumps.

If you have the space, put large-leafed hostas in the background and small-leafed ones in the foreground as ground fillers.

My favourite amongst the small-leafed varieties is *H. tardiana* 'Halcyon', which has blue leaves. Other short varieties are *H.* 'See Saw' and *H.* 'Elf', which grow to 25cm (10in) tall.

These plants are suitable for the "second row".

Houttuynia

Terribly rampant. But then, that may be what you are looking for: a splendid area of white-flowering plants that have green or flecked leaves. A normal back garden can be really full of them, and yet tranquillity and suspense can still be created as long as some good single plants are placed in amongst them. As thick hedges they are useful as partitions. It is a perfect plant for a boring entrance with grass, next to the drive, for example, or in front of the house with flowering and fruit-bearing bushes, some box globes and ferns in between. The coloured variety is called *H. cordata* 'Chameleon' and has many yellow, red, and green colours in its leaves.

Hypericum androsaemum

This grows to 80cm (32in) tall and is an easy, thick ground-cover plant that has yellow flowers and red berries and is bare in the winter. It can live with *Pachysandra* and *Waldsteinia. Hypericum calcycinum* is also a ground-cover plant. It can continue to grow rampant beside *Pachysandra* because it also has underground shoots.The flowers are yellow, large, and striking, and the leaves are fresh green. In principle it is evergreen in a protected garden; after a winter with a great deal of frost the leaves go brown and it is best to trim off all the little brown branches and wait for the new shoots with green leaves.

Hyssopus (hyssop)

A blue, flowering herb that grows to about 40cm (16in) and needs sun. The flowers are blue, white, or pink, depending on the variety. Trim the

plant in the late spring with hedge clippers and an evenly growing covering of blue flowers will appear in May, June, and July. The blue hyssop is called *H. officinalis*, the white *H. o.* 'Albus', and the pink *H. o.* 'Roseus'.

Iris pumila

Put these plants in a fine layer of gravel or shingle, which fills up the space between the plants. If you do not do this you will get a lot of weeds growing between the plants in the first years, which involves work. However, if you once decide to let a thick group of *I. pumila* expand in a sunny spot, you will have a spectacular array of sword-shaped leaves and attractive iris flowers.

Lamium (deadnettle)

This nettle-like plant does not sting,

which is possibly why this group of wild plants is so popular.
Lamium maculatum likes shade. In the wild it occurs in woods. The yellow deadnettle is also called *Lamiastrum*; there are several varieties of these on sale, for example *Lamiastrum galeobdolon* 'Herman's Pride', which has silvery flecked leaves and numerous yellow flowers.

 L. g. 'Variegatum' has silver variegated leaves and yellow flowers. The plant called *Lamium* is very much like *Lamiastrum* as regards foliage and growth, although the stems are sometimes rather less rampant and long. *Lamium maculatum* 'Roseum' has pink flowers with large flower calyxes. *L. m.* 'Beacon Silver' has silvery leaves and purple flowers and *L. m.* 'Album' has white flowers.

Lavandula (lavender)

A half-shrub equally at home with shrubs or perennials. Plant them in a sunny spot and in bulk as a ground-cover plant and you will be surprised at the effect. This is not something original, but it is not often seen. Put a white single bush rose amongst them, such as *Rosa* 'Marie Pavic,' to give a colour contrast. Or plant the pink and white rose *R.* 'Lady of the Dawn' with it, which keeps blooming continuously and likes sun. *Geranium psilostemon* can also be planted between as a lilac-violet cloud of brightly coloured flowers. There is white lavender, *L. angustifolia* 'Alba', there is a lavender-blue variety, *L. a.* 'Grappen-hall', and a pink one, *L. a.* 'Hidcote Pink'. So there is plenty of choice for your colour range. Another acquisi-tion for the border is Spanish

The yucca is also winter hardy in this climate and provides a good contrast in the border with its unusual leaf shape.

lavender, *L. stoechas*, which has violet-blue flowers that are quite different. I have seen them in Corsica in the wild, and enjoy the large groups of greenish-grey leaves with fat buds from which small flag-like petals emerge in my garden in Zeeland.

Mentha rotundifolia 'Variegata' (variegated mint)

A magnificent perennial herb which has whitish-green leaves with great decorative value and which expands considerably. Plant it under bushes or under tallish bush roses.

Mertensia

Blooms a magnificent bright speed-well blue with long, slightly hanging trumpet-shaped flowers that also have a touch of pink in their flower trumpets. *M. asiatica* stays at 20cm (8in), so is really short, while

M. pterocarpa grows a little taller. They are both striking summer-flowering plants for sun and half-shade.

Nepeta (catmint)

Cats love rolling around in these plants. If this annoys you, put cock-tail sticks among the plants and the cats will go to lie in their owners' *Nepeta*! *N. faassenii* 'Six Hills Giant' blooms for a long time, which may be the reason it has acquired this heroic name. The leaves are grey, and it is an ideal sun-lover for a low bed with its blue flowers and its grey aura. It also withstands dry conditions.

Oenothera (evening primrose)

Grows very tall in the wild, at least 2m (6ft). *O. missouriensis* is short and has large yellow bells which are sometimes just right for fitting into a

colour scheme. Plant them in full sunlight and put some other yellow-leafed plants, something blue, or more yellowy-green flowering plants and single plants with them. It is a bright colour and therefore suitable for sturdy gardens.

Origanum

Besides *Origanum vulgare*, the wild marjoram, there are many splendid varieties and species, so this plant has a right to be included. *O. rotundifolium* and the *O. vulgare* varieties are all short, about 25cm (20in) tall. The colours are always purple-pink, but the shape of both the flower and the leaves differs.

Pachysandra terminalis

Has leaves like strawberry leaves, with a small stem from which five small leaves grow. They are a glossy

fresh green and distinctly elongated. The leaves grow more or less horizontally and, because the plant makes rhizomes, it is an ideal ground-cover plant that soon covers large surfaces. Plant young plants about 20cm (8in) apart and the ground will be covered in two years. The more thickly you plant, the more quickly this happens. Because the plant is evergreen it provides a splendid winter scene. It flowers white in early summer, and is cheerful without being oppressive or too striking.

Phlox subulata

Stays short and looks like the wild phlox from Pennsylvania which I saw there at the edge of the woods. There are many varieties of *Phlox subulata*, which all reach 15cm (6in) in height when in flower, so they are definitely creepers. *P.* 'Maischnee'

blooms in May and is white, *P.* 'Marjorie' is purple-pink, while *P.* 'Moerheimii' is pink. They are attractive plants to have in beds, along edges, or right at the front of a perennial border, or as ground-cover plants for larger areas with an ornamental grass, a fanciful bush, or a rose standing out above them.

Polygonatum (Solomon's seal)

Another of my favourite woodland plants. A short stem appears with little white hanging bells underneath two leaves, which stick out like wings. The leaves and the flower together look rather like a dragon-fly. A whole field of them is the most beautiful thing I can imagine in deep shade, at least in flower; after that the combined effect is one of tranquillity and it gives good ground cover because not many other things will

grow as well so deep in the shade. The leaves of *P. multiflorum* grow to a height of 50cm (20in). There are also magnificent taller species.

Polygonum (knotweed)

A garden weed which appears on ground as soon as it is left bare. There are magnificent cultivated forms of this weed, which, though in itself quite splendid, no one wants because of its predeliction to come up in all the places where we do not want it. Hence the cultivated species and varieties, which stay neatly in their place – at least most of them do. The wide *P. bistorta* spreads rapidly and likes to take over the whole ground with its large elongated leaves and its slender stems with spiky light pink flowers. There are several varieties of this. *P. affine* is an easy ground-cover plant which stays

Artemisia is grey, Digitalis *is white, and so are the delphiniums in the background.*
Above: White-flowering Agapanthus.
Left: André van den Eerenbeemt designed this town garden in 's-Hertogenbosch.
Opposite page: Great Dixter's famous border garden.

short and has deep pink flowers.
P. a. 'Darjeeling Red' is deep pinky red, and *P. a.* 'Superbum' is pink and is the one which keeps flowering most abundantly.

Pulmonaria (lungwort)

A wild woodland plant. Lungwort likes moisture and a certain amount of lime, which is apparent if you look at their natural growing places. This good woodland plant blooms in the spring. There are green-leafed species which are boring in the summer but do flower beautifully. I always recommend choosing a flecked-leafed variety, such as *P. saccharata* 'Sissinghurst White', which produces short, whitish-green leaves. There are also good long-leafed species, *P. longifolia,* which I have already described with the foliage plants. Collect them; they are

indispensable for pink, white, and particularly blue in the spring.

Salvia nemorosa 'Blauhügel'

Grows to a height of 40cm (16in) and belongs among lavender and hyssop as regards appearance. If you compose a whole blue garden with them, with three species of plants, this will be dazzling, fascinating, and exciting. Cut off the flowers when they have finished blooming, and another slightly smaller wave of blue flower spikes will follow.

Santolina

Belongs in southern gardens. There are many different leaf colours of this half-shrub, which is easy to prune but which is always classified as a weed. *S. chamaecyparissus* 'Edward Bowles' grows to a height of 40cm (16in) and has creamy-yellow

flowers which appear on the stems as sturdy buds. *S.* 'Lambrook Silver' has bright silver-coloured leaves and also has creamy-yellow flowers.

Scutellaria

Usually quite tall with lip-shaped flowers. It is a permanent inhabitant of the garden. *S. incana,* at 80cm (32in), is too tall for this chapter, but there is also *S. alpina,* which grows to 20cm (8in) tall and will bloom in the colours purple, blue, and white.

Sedum acre

A small curly plant with tiny yellow stars that makes no demands at all of the ground. It prefers to be on stony ground, where it is dry and there is little competition from rampant-growing grasses. If you like other tints, particularly white and pink, you will enjoy other short *Sedum,* as

long as the situation is sunny. *S. album* 'Coral Carpet', for example, also remains short and has evergreen leaves which go a purple colour. The flowers are white. Many ground-cover *Sedum* species and varieties are to be found in the rock garden department. I frequently use *S. spurium* 'Schorbusser Blut', which has deep pink-violet flowers and is splendid in combination with the perennial *Fuchsia magellanica*, *Rosa* 'Betty Prior', and *Polygonum amplexicaule*. The other *Sedum* which I use as ground cover is the yellow *S. kamtschaticum*. *S.* 'Herbstfreude' can form very large, taller groups, for example with bushes of *Buddleja*, which would be wonderful for buzzing bees. It is an ultra-sturdy *Sedum* which you can plant in large amounts in the sun, if you have room. It will keep on flowering abundantly.

Tellima

The leaves are quite coarse but fresh green, and long stems emerge from them with little greeny-yellow bells. A whole area of *Tellima* can be rather untidy, so limit the group to within a border; this is not quite so easy because they grow wildly. If you have room next to a drive or under rhododendrons that have finished flowering, you will be happy with them and the ground will be covered elegantly.

Tiarella

T. cordifolia and *T. wherryi* cover the ground with felty light green leaves which are very fluffy. Little white spikes emerge from them, which go on flowering for the whole summer. It is a favourite for a delicate garden, and is good as a contrast with a few heavy plant groups and single plants, such as holly, *Taxus*, *Viburnum*, and roses, because a substantial area of them is everything you can imagine in the way of delicacy.

Thymus (thyme)

Well known in the wild. There are also many slightly taller species, which vary from country to country. In Crete you see actual bushes of it; in northern Europe they appear as creepers amongst the grass or other verge flowers. *T. citriodorus* 'Silver Queen' is a silver-leafed variety with silvery-green foliage and a lilac-pink flower.

There is also a yellow variegated thyme and of course *T. vulgaris*, which grows to a height of 30cm (12in) and is strong in slightly drier places but also does well in my garden on the damp clay.

139

Tussilago farfara (coltsfoot)

This is a plant for large surfaces because it grows rampant. It has splendid green foliage and, of course, the first little wild flowers to appear – rather daisy-like and bright yellow. Coltsfoot is wonderful for anyone who has the space and likes experimenting.

Veronica filiformis (speedwell)

There is scarcely a prettier flowering plant, even though the flower is so small that many gardeners do not warrant this little weed a glance – which is a pity. I leave it until the other plants have grown large and then pull it out, which is easy to do. There are many short varieties for the sun: *V. austriaca* 'Ionian Skies' is sky blue and grows to a height of 30cm (12in), the same height as the familiar *V. a.* 'Shirley Blue'. The very shortest

is the creeping *V.* 'Madame Mercier' which is 5cm (2in) tall and has light blue flowers – a wonderful little plant.

Viola (pansy)

There are so many *Viola cornuta* hybrids which flower in delicate or bright colours and thrive in the sun that there would be a whole list, so I will mention the ones I use most frequently: *V.* 'Amethyst' is soft violet, *V.* 'White Superior' and *V.* 'John Wallmark' are light and dark lilac, *V.* ''Boughton Blue' is grey-blue, *V.* 'Moonlight' is soft yellow, and *V.* 'Mollie Sanderson' is black, which goes well with grey and green.

Waldsteinia ternata

Has leaves like strawberries but they are dull and more curly. It is a flat ground-cover plant, which, if possible, grows even shorter than

Annuals such as Gaillardia, Begonia, *and* Salvia *have been brought together here in a sparkling Aladdin's cave.*

Pachysandra. It prefers to be in a sunny place, while *Pachysandra* stays fresher in the shade and goes yellowish in the sun. So it is good planted under bushes with *Waldsteinia* next to it in the sun. However, you must separate the plants carefully by means of a path or other barrier, as *Pachysandra* will overgrow *Waldsteinia* with its root shoots. Another possibility is to plant roses which do not grow too tall, such as *Rosa* 'Mozart', *R.* 'Schubert', or *R.* 'Ballerina', which are all faded lilac. Instead of the partition you can plant *Hypericum*, which can form the transition from rampant-growing ground-cover plants to the boundary of the garden.

Photo credits

A. J. van der Horst:
title page, pp. 6 (right), 8 (top), 9, 10, 12 (top), 14, 15, 16, 17 (left), 18 (top), 19 (top), 22, 23, 24 (bottom), 25, 26, 29, 32 (top), 35, 37, 38, 40, 43 (top), 44 (left), 45, 46, 47, 49, 50, 51, 52, 53, 55, 56, 57, 58, 59, 60, 62, 63, 66, 67, 69, 70, 72, 74 (right), 75, 76 (top), 78, 80 (top) 81, 82, 83, 84 (bottom), 85 (right), 86 (top), 90 (top), 92, 93, 94, 95, 96 (bottom), 97, 98, 99, 100 (left), 102 (top), 103, 104 (top), 105, 106, 107, 108, 110, 112, 113, 114, 117, 118, 119, 120, 121 (left), 122, 123, 126 (top), 127, 128, 129 (left and bottom right), 130, 131, 132 (left), 133, 134, 135, 136, 139, 140, 142

M. Kurpershoek:
pp. 6 (left), 7, 12 (bottom), 31 (right), 34 (right), 39, 43 (bottom), 65, 71, 85 (left), 86 (bottom), 87, 89, 91, 109, 116 (top), 125, 129 (top right), 137

G. Otter:
pp. 30 (bottom), 41, 42, 48, 54, 64, 76 (bottom), 80 (bottom), 84 (top), 90 (bottom), 96 (top), 100 (right), 104 (bottom), 115, 121 (right), 126 (bottom), 132 (bottom right)

N. Vermeulen:
pp. 8 (bottom), 11 (top and bottom), 17 (right), 18 (bottom), 19 (bottom), 20, 21, 24 (top), 28, 30 (top), 31 (left), 32 bottom), 34 (left), 36, 44 (right), 61, 68, 74 (left), 88, 101, 102 (bottom), 111, 116 (bottom), 132 (top right)

Thanks are due to Mrs Van Bennekom, Domburg; Cleen Lelie, Voorne; Mrs Dekker, Veere: Castle Gardens, Arcen; the Poley family, Nisse; Priona Gardens, Schuinesloot.